WHAT A YEAR IT WAS!
1957

A walk back in time to revisit
what life was like in the year that
has special meaning for you...

*Congratulations
and
Best Wishes*

To

From

DEDICATION

To My Daughter Laurie Whose Support, Commitment And Endless Hours Of Hard Work Made This Book Possible.

Designer • Peter Hess
Researcher • Laurie Cohn

CONTENTS

POLITICS
&WORLD
EVENTS

President Eisenhower Inaugurated For Second Term.

His Inaugural Speech Is A Plea For Peace Among All Nations.

"...May the turbulence of our age yield to the true time of peace when men and nations shall share a life that honors the dignity of each..."

President Eisenhower Is Inaugurated For A Second Term As Leader Of Not Only America, But Of All Free People, And Pledges Use Of Armed Forces Against Soviet Aggression In The Middle East.

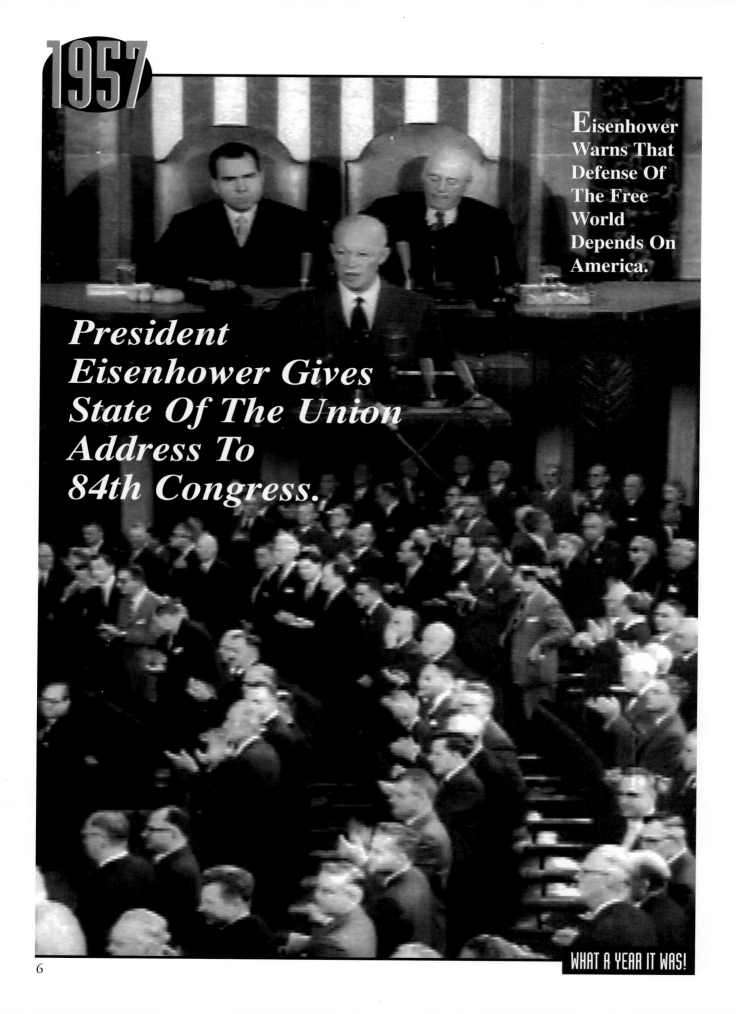

1957

Eisenhower Warns That Defense Of The Free World Depends On America.

President Eisenhower Gives State Of The Union Address To 84th Congress.

EGYPTIAN/ISRAELI IMPASSE DELAYS OPENING OF THE SUEZ CANAL

President Eisenhower, vacationing at the Georgia plantation of Secretary of The Treasury Humphreys, calls an emergency meeting of his top advisors, Henry Cabot Lodge (right), John Foster Dulles (left) and Humphreys (far right), to discuss the Mid-East crisis. At the heart of the problem is the Suez Canal.

The President is apprised of the deteriorating situation by Secretary of State Dulles. The gravity of the Egyptian impasse causes him to cut short his winter holiday and return to Washington.

"Planeta Genova," a small Italian tanker is turned back by the Egyptians as it tries to make its way through the Canal.

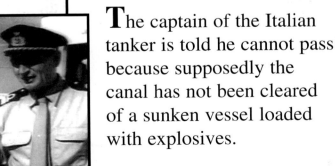

The captain of the Italian tanker is told he cannot pass because supposedly the canal has not been cleared of a sunken vessel loaded with explosives.

1957

NIXON VISITS HUNGARIAN

Mr. Nixon Is Welcomed By Austrian Dignitaries On His Inspection Trip To Hungarian Refugee Centers.

His trip includes visits to all the major collection points where refugees await their final destination.

REFUGEE CAMPS IN AUSTRIA
— SEEKS SPEEDIER AID FOR REFUGES

21,000 refugees are authorized to enter the United States, but Nixon is convinced the number should be increased.

Old and young they have come to these refugee centers seeking freedom and to try to convince Nixon that America should expand its quota.

Vice President Richard Nixon and Tracey Vorhees, who heads the refugee program, arrive for a meeting with President Eisenhower after Nixon's trip to Austria.

Nixon gives Eisenhower a report on the results of his inspection trip. His recommendation is more help for those who gave all for liberty.

1957

President Eisenhower Suffers Mild Stroke.

 Eisenhower Proposes International Arms Control

House Of Representatives Passes Watered Down Version Of Civil Rights Bill 72-18. Eisenhower Tells Senate He'd Rather Have No Bill Than The One That Passed.

President Eisenhower Signs Niagra Power Bill Authorizing Construction Of Hydroelectric Dam.

THE U.S. SUPREME COURT

...Upholds Ban On Sale Of Obscene Literature. Justices William O. Douglas And Hugo Black Cast Dissenting Votes.

...Rules That A License To Practice Law May Not Be Refused On The Grounds Of Past Association With The Communist Party.

★★★★★★★★★★★★★★

★★★★★★★★★★★★★★

U.S. MILITARY FORCE REDUCED BY 100,000 TROOPS BY SECRETARY OF DEFENSE WILSON.

U.S. State Department Refuses To Validate Eleanor Roosevelt's Passport For A Visit To Communist China.

Nine Democratic Women Hold Seats In The House Of Representatives.

Democrats Win Major Contest In Off-Year Elections.

 **Estes Kefauver Loses Foreign Relations Committee Seat To Senator John F. Kennedy.**

WHAT A YEAR IT WAS!

Teamster Corruption Investigated By U.S. Senate.

Teamster V.P. Jimmy Hoffa Arrested By FBI On Bribery Charges.

Jimmy Hoffa Indicted On Charges Of Bribery, Conspiracy And Obstruction Of Justice For Trying To Get Senate Committee Files.

Expelled AFL-CIO Head Dave Beck Charged With Income Tax Evasion.

Teamsters Union Expelled From AFL-CIO When Jimmy Hoffa, With The Full Backing Of The Union, Refuses To Purge The Union Of Criminals.

Jimmy Hoffa Acquitted On Bribery Charges.

New York Mayor Robert F. Wagner, Jr. Wins Re-Election By A Record Margin Of Over 919,000 Votes While Traditionally Republican Up-State New York Goes Democrat Electing Five New Mayors.

William Proxmire, The First Democrat To Be Elected To The U.S. Senate In The State Of Wisconsin In 25 Years, Wins The Seat Vacated By The Death Of Joseph R. McCarthy.

U.S. Communist Party Votes To Be Independent Of Soviet Control.

SOUTHERN

Richard Nixon

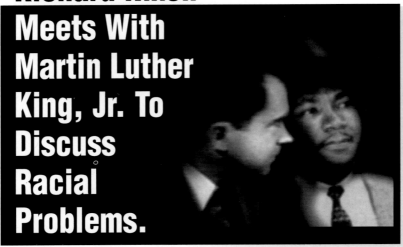

Meets With Martin Luther King, Jr. To Discuss Racial Problems.

FLORIDA GOVERNOR COLLINS SUSPENDS BUS SERVICE TO THWART INTEGRATION EFFORT.

INTERRACIAL ATHLETIC EVENTS OUTLAWED BY GEORGIA LEGISLATURE.

Despite A Record Filibuster From Senator Strom Thurmond, The Right-Wing South Carolina Democrat, The First Major Civil Rights Bill Since The Reconstruction Era Was Passed By The Senate Under The Leadership Of Democratic Leader, Lyndon B. Johnson. The Bill Not Only Assures Voting Rights For Negroes* And Other Minorities, It Also Creates A Civil Rights Commission.

Bomb Rips Through Nashville School That Admitted Negroes*.

Negro* Minister In Birmingham Beaten By Mob As He Tries To Enter A Group Of Children, Including His Daughter, Into An All-White School.

*Negro was the commonly used term in 1957.

12

DISCOMFORT

Arkansas Governor Orval Faubus Deploys State Police As School Integration Begins.

Acting Under Governor Faubus' Orders, Arkansas National Guard Bars Nine Negroes* From Entering Little Rock's All-White Central High School.

President Eisenhower, After Conferring With Attorney General Herbert Brownell, Signs Emergency Proclamation Calling On All Persons To Cease And Desist From Obstructing Justice By Interfering With The Enforcement Of A Federal Court Order For The Integration Of Central High School. The Arkansas National Guard Is Federalized And Troops Dispatched To Little Rock Where, With Fixed Bayonets, They Escort The Nine Children Into School.

President Eisenhower And Governor Faubus Meet To Discuss School Integration.

1,500 WHITES DESCEND ON THE HIGH SCHOOL IN VIOLENT PROTEST AGAINST ADMITTANCE OF THE NEGRO* CHILDREN. MOB FORCES THE NEGRO* CHILDREN OUT OF SCHOOL.

1957

Russian Spy Arrested In Brooklyn

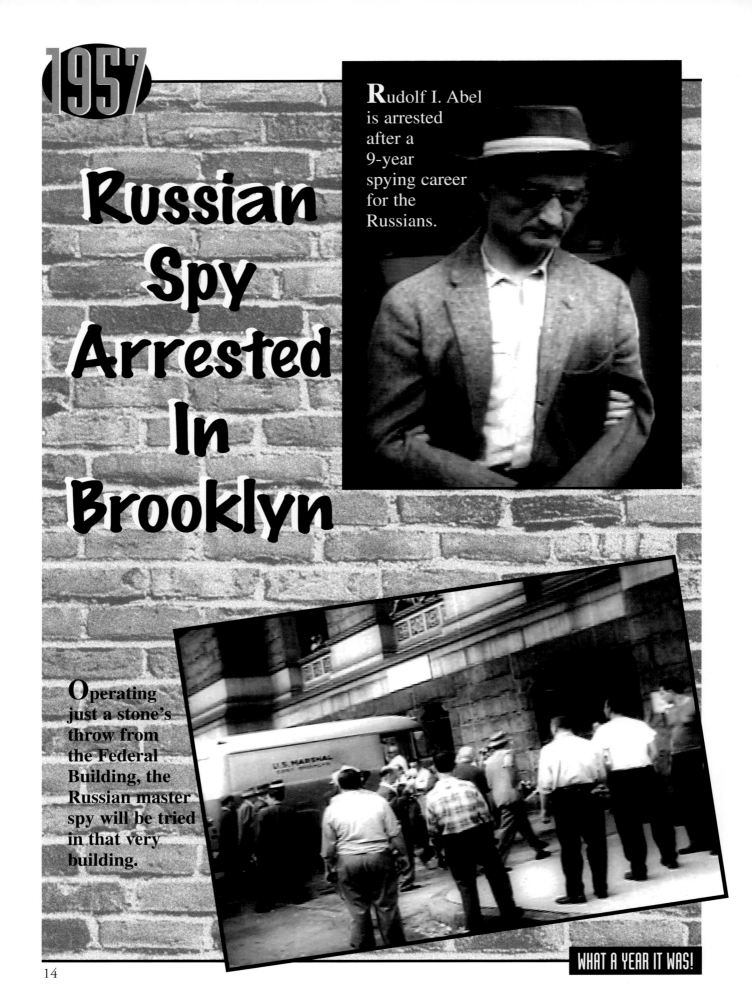

Rudolf I. Abel is arrested after a 9-year spying career for the Russians.

Operating just a stone's throw from the Federal Building, the Russian master spy will be tried in that very building.

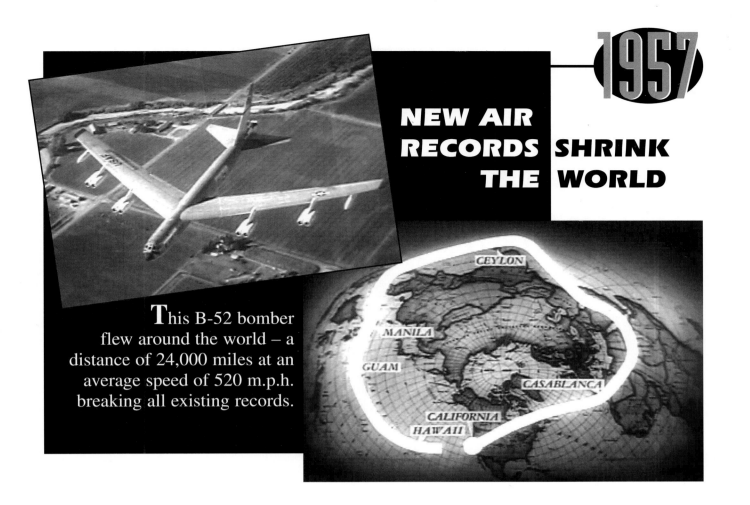

1957

NEW AIR RECORDS SHRINK THE WORLD

This B-52 bomber flew around the world – a distance of 24,000 miles at an average speed of 520 m.p.h. breaking all existing records.

CEYLON

MANILA

GUAM

CASABLANCA

CALIFORNIA
HAWAII

GEN. CURTIS LE MAY
Breaks Non-Stop Record

The jets fly 11,000 miles non-stop from Massachusetts to Buenos Aires in record time of 13 hours, 2 minutes, 51 seconds at a speed of 450 m.p.h.

General Curtis E. Le May getting ready to lead a group of jet Strato-Tankers.

1957

PRIME MINISTER ANTHONY EDEN REPLACED BY HAROLD MACMILLAN

Britain's Prime Minister Anthony Eden's Career Ends After Only 21 Months In Office, One Of The Shortest For A Prime Minister In Britain's History. The Tragedy Of The Suez Invasion And Ill Health Brought About His Resignation.

Queen Elizabeth II replaces Prime Minister Anthony Eden with Harold Macmillan, leader of the right wing Conservative Party who will now have to face Britain's many financial problems and shrinking colonial empire.

Harold Macmillan, son of an American mother, will carry on the tradition of 10 Downing Street.

Germany's Chancellor Adenauer Returned To Office

In an overwhelming vote of confidence, the Republic of Germany returns 81-year old Chancellor Adenauer (lft) and his government to office.

Enthusiastic well-wishers greet the Chancellor.

In Canada an upset election ousted Prime Minister Louis St. Laurent and his Liberal government ending his party's 22-year rule.

Winning by a narrow margin, newly installed Prime Minister Diefenbaker and his Conservative Party will be dealing with Canada's expanding economy and industry.

CANADA'S UPSET ELECTION

1957

CRISIS IN JORDAN
MARTIAL LAW DECLARED
6TH FLEET STANDS BY

A young man stands guard outside the palace.

The world focuses its attention on the royal palace in Amman, Jordan.

The young King Hussein, facing a political crisis, struggles to keep his nation intact but failing to reach a political solution declares martial law.

Loyal Bedouin sheiks pledge their allegiance to Hussein.

With the first test of President Eisenhower's Middle East doctrine, he proclaims Jordan's independence to be vital.

Implementing the doctrine, heavy elements of the 6th fleet are ordered to sea under sealed orders for a show of force.

WHAT A YEAR IT WAS!

THE SUEZ CANAL IS CLEARED FOR PASSAGE

The last obstacle in the Suez Canal, the tug Edgar Bonet, is raised near the midway point of the waterway.

Removal of the craft, scuttled five months ago by Egypt, clears the way for passage in the near future although the questions of tolls and control have still not been resolved.

U.N. engineer Wheeler and Commander Byrnes observe the removal.

INDEPENDENCE DAY CELEBRATION IN GREECE

The highlight of the parade is young Prince Constantine's first official appearance with his father.

The King and Queen of Greece lead the parade celebrating Greece Independence Day.

Greece's modern army organized with the help of General Van Fleet during the Communist uprising presents a compact striking force.

As a member of NATO, Greece occupies a strategic position in the Mediterranean during the present Mid-East unrest.

WHAT A YEAR IT WAS!

A NEW NATION IS BORN IN AFRICA

Vice President and Mrs. Nixon are in Africa to attend ceremonies celebrating Ghana's independence from Britain.

Jubilant natives perform their tribal dance.

Patriot Nkrumah Kwame (rt.) pictured with Harlem's Adam Clayton Powell is the first president of the former British Colony of the Gold Coast.

The move to African self-rule is established.

Your heart will be glad you came by DC-7

Whatever your reason for getting there sooner...

Take the **DC-7**__world's fastest airliner

With its top speed a remarkable 410 miles an hour, the DC-7 wings you with velvet swiftness across the oceans, across the continents—anywhere in the world!

There's unbeatable luxury and comfort, too. The spacious DC-7 cabin is pressurized, air conditioned, sound-proofed and tastefully appointed to make your travel completely restful.

Next trip, get there *sooner*, more *comfortably*—by DC-7. See why *more* people and *more* airlines fly Douglas than all other airplanes *combined!*

DOUGLAS
BUILDERS OF THE DC-8 JETLINER

Aga Khan, Mega Millionaire Leader Of 40 Million Ismaili Moslems, Dies At 80.

Mourners gather to pay tribute to their beloved leader.

Before his death, the Aga Khan chose his 20-year old grandson, Karim Khan, to be his successor.

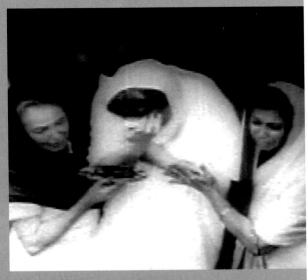

The Aga Khan's French wife mourns the loss of her husband.

Philippine President Ramón Magsaysay, Patriot And Leader Of His People, Found Dead In Plane Crash On Island Of Cebu.

WHAT A YEAR IT WAS!

1957

Missile to Missile

First U.S. Civilian Atomic Power Plant Goes Into Operation In Shippingport, Pa.

The First Test Of An Atlas Intercontinental Missile Ends In Failure When It Explodes Shortly After Take-Off From Its Launching Site In Cape Canaveral, Florida.

James R. Killian, Jr. Named Special Aid For Space Technology By President Eisenhower.

U.S. Unveils Plan To Install Intermediate-Range Missiles In Western Europe.

U.S. Fails In Three Attempts To Fire Rocket 3,000 Miles Into Space.

U.S. Successfully Tests Intermediate-Range Ballistic Missile Jupiter.

U.S. Launches The U.S.S. Skate In Groton, Connecticut-Its Third Atomic Powered Submarine.

Navy Launches Rocket With Satellite Instruments 126 Miles Into Space.

THOR INTERMEDIATE-RANGE MISSILES TO BE PRODUCED BY AIR FORCE.

Nuclear Test Series Set Off In Yucca Flat, Nevada By U.S. Atomic Energy Commission Including First Underground Test.

The Soviet Union Launches Sputnik, The First Man-Made Satellite, Into Orbit Around The Earth. President Eisenhower Addresses Nation To Allay Fears Concerning The Soviet's Scientific Achievements.

In A Pact With The U.S., Soviets Agree To Place Earth Satellite And All Pilotless Missiles Under International Control. 22 Nations Support U.S. Plan To Limit Outer Space Exploration To Peaceful Purposes Only.

THE ARMY AIR DEFENSE COMMAND ISSUES REPORT THAT NEW YORK AND OTHER MAJOR AMERICAN CITIES WILL BE DEFENDED BY NIKE HERCULES MISSILES WITH ATOMIC WARHEADS.

Soviets Launch Lenin, First Nuclear Ice-Breaker.

Asserting Soviet Missile Superiority, Khrushchev Challenges U.S. To Rocket-Range Shooting Match.

International Atomic Energy Agency Is Formed.

The Soviets Become The First Nation To Ratify International Atomic Energy Agency Charter.

U. S. S. R.

Andrei Gromyko Replaces Dmitri T. Shepilov As Soviet Foreign Minister.

China's Chou En-lai Visits Moscow.

As A Warning To Western Europe Against Nuclear War, The Soviet Union Tests Another H-Bomb.

In A Move To Decentralize Russian Industry, Khrushchev Creates 92 Industrial Regions.

Soviets Agree To Western Plan For Atomic Test Ban.

Soviet Leader Khrushchev Promises Elevation Of Soviet Standard Of Living Stating: "Marxism-Leninism Will Taste Better With Butter."

Tito And Khrushchev Meet In Belgrade Pledging Closer Ties.

Two U.S. Diplomats Expelled From Moscow On Charges Of Spying.

Soviet War Hero Marshal Georgi Zhukov Stripped Of All Power.

First Russian Warships To Use The Suez Canal Since 1917 Pass Through The Waterway.

Members Of The Soviet U.N. Delegation Land At McGuire Air Force Base In New Jersey In First Soviet Civilian Plane To Touch Down In The United States.

CUBA & FIDEL CASTRO

Cuban Rebel Leader Fidel Castro Wages Fight Against Fulgencio Batista Regime From Secret Jungle Outpost.

Castro Interviewed On CBS Documentary On Cuban Revolution.

Cuba's President Batista Suspends All Constitutional Guarantees In Response To Outbreak Of Anti-Government Violence.

Castro Joined By Cuban Soldiers In Fighting South Of Havana.

Cuban President Batista Will Not Seek Re-Election.

The Headlines

Saudi Arabia's King Saud Visits Washington With Son On Official Visit.

Agreement Regulating Seal Hunting Ratified By The U.S., Soviet Union, Canada And Japan.

U.S. Continues Its Policy Of Non-Recognition Of Red China.

Benito Mussolini's Widow Receives Permission From The Italian Government To Exhume The Coffin Of Il Duce To Hold A Funeral.

François Duvalier Elected President Of Haiti.

French And British Banks Nationalized By Egypt.

Egypt Bars Israel Access To The Suez Canal And Saudi Arabia Cuts Off Gulf Of Aqaba.

Kashmir Becomes Indian State.

American Occupation Headquarters In Japan Is Dismantled.

The U.N. Demands Complete And Unconditional Israeli Withdrawal From The Gaza Strip. Thousands Of Israelis Protest.

Israel Withdraws From The Gaza Strip.

Indonesian President Sukarno Escapes Assassination Attempt In Jakarta.

With U.S. Backing In The Form Of $10 Million In Foreign Aid, Jordan's King Hussein Leads Military Coup Ousting Pro-Egyptian Sympathizers In Government.

Israel Offers To Negotiate With Arabs On Refugee Problem.

Archbishop Makarios Is Released By The British Who Bar Him From Cyprus.

Egypt, Saudi Arabia And Syria Sign Accord To Replace British Aid To Jordan.

Jordan Closes Embassy In Cairo.

Announcement From Jerusalem On The Fall Of Premier David Ben Gurion's Coalition Government.

A Grenade Attack Injures Israeli Premier David Ben-Gurion Along With Four Cabinet Members.

Hungary Institutes Death Penalty For Strikes And Other Acts Of Civil Disobedience.

Three Leaders Of The Hungarian Uprising Sentenced To Death.

Ireland Elects Eamon de Valera As Prime Minister.

French Government Tries To Restore Peace In Algiers.

GREAT BRITAIN

◆ QUEEN ELIZABETH II OPENS CANADIAN PARLIAMENT, THE FIRST REIGNING MONARCH TO DO SO. THEN ON TO THE U.S. FOR STATE FUNCTIONS INCLUDING VISIT TO WILLIAMSBURG, THE FIRST BRITISH SETTLEMENT.

◆ QUEEN ELIZABETH II ABOLISHES PRESENTATION AT COURT FOR DEBUTANTES.

◆ WOMEN TO SIT IN BRITAIN'S HOUSE OF LORDS FOR THE FIRST TIME IN HISTORY.

◆ MALAYA, THE LAST OF BRITAIN'S ASIAN COLONIES, WINS INDEPENDENCE AND ELECTS FIRST RULER, SIR ABDUL RAHMAN.

◆ PHILIP, DUKE OF EDINBURGH, BECOMES PRINCE OF THE UNITED KINGDOM IN AN ACT BY HIS WIFE, QUEEN ELIZABETH II.

◆ GREAT BRITAIN GRANTS AUTONOMY TO NIGERIA.

NOBEL PEACE PRIZE

Lester B. Pearson
(Canada)

ARRIVALS

Princess Caroline Of Monaco & Caroline Kennedy

PASSINGS

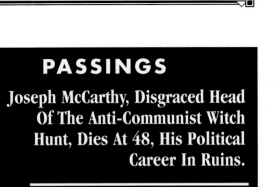

Joseph McCarthy, Disgraced Head Of The Anti-Communist Witch Hunt, Dies At 48, His Political Career In Ruins.

King Haakon VII Of Norway Dies At 85 Succeeded By His 54 Year Old Son, Olaf V.

Zagreb, Yugoslavia Is The Site Of One Of The First U.S. Style Supermarkets To Open In The Eastern Bloc.

Adenauer Victor In German Election By Landslide.

The sphere above is a "core" for one kind of research atomic reactor. The metal tubes in the foreground and at the right show various test designs for holding the small uranium fuel pellets in other kinds of atomic reactors.

Strange new "tools" of atomic-electric power

These are some of the strange new "tools" used to produce, test, or experiment with atomic-electric power. They are among the things that will help bring electricity from the atom.

"Tools" like these are being used in developing several atomic-electric plants now under way. A number of electric light and power companies from many parts of the country are working with each other and with equipment manufacturers and the Atomic Energy Commission to develop the plants.

For more than 75 years, America's independent electric light and power companies have supplied more and more electricity to this growing nation. Today they produce more than any other single nation in the world. And they have helped develop ways to produce it more efficiently year after year. That's why you can expect electric companies to continue to do their part to advance the new science of producing electricity from the atom.

America's Independent Electric Light and Power Companies*

*Company names on request through this magazine

28

PEOPLE

President And Mrs. Eisenhower Kick Off Holiday Season With Traditional Lighting Of The White House Tree

With a flick of a wrist the 80-foot spruce is illuminated with 9,000 lights.

President and Mrs. Eisenhower join Richard and Pat Nixon for the Annual Tree-Lighting ceremony.

Thousands of invited guests share in this joyous occasion.

Marlon Brando Makes A Plea For Contributions To The International Rescue Committee To Aid Hungarian Refugees.

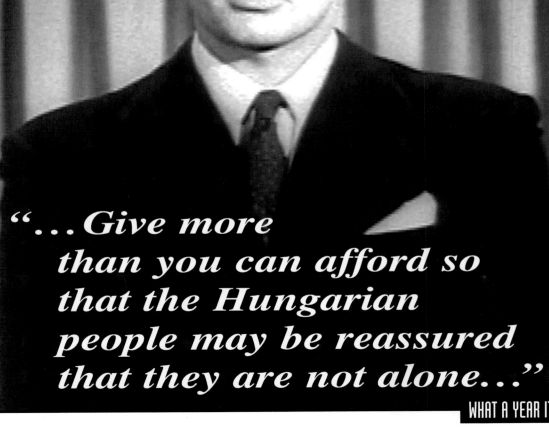

"...Give more than you can afford so that the Hungarian people may be reassured that they are not alone..."

Dublin's Jewish Mayor Visits Ike

1957

Ireland's unofficial ambassador, Jewish Lord Mayor of Dublin Robert Briscoe, visits with Ike at the White House for an informal half hour.

Mayor Briscoe thanks Ike for the kind reception he received in America and for the gift of Irish cut glass, green of course.

THE MAD BOMBER IS CAUGHT AFTER A 15-YEAR BOMB SPREE

A fifteen-year reign of terror ends in New York when George Metesky (center) is captured.

The Mad Bomber admits to bombing 21 public places for revenge.

PUMPS A TON OF FISH A MINUTE FROM BOAT TO SHORE!

RIPLEY'S

FISHING BOATS AT A WEST COAST SARDINE CANNERY AVOID WHARFSIDE "TRAFFIC JAMS" AND DELIVER CATCHES HOURS FRESHER. THEY UNLOAD INTO A FLOATING TANK 1000 FEET OFFSHORE. THE FISH ARE THEN SUCKED TO SHORE THROUGH A LARGE PIPE BY A POWERFUL FISH PUMP. SPECIALLY DESIGNED BY B-W'S BYRON JACKSON, THIS PUMP PULLS IN A TON OF SARDINES AND 950 GALLONS OF SEA WATER EVERY 60 SECONDS. FISH SHOOT RIGHT THROUGH THE PUMP, YET IT DOESN'T EVEN BRUISE THEM.

1957 NORGE TIMELINE AUTOMATIC WASHER

"AUTOMATIC" WASHER OF THE 1850's RAN ON ONE WIFEPOWER!

THE WORK-SAVING PROVIDED BY THIS "CLOTHES CHURN" WAS QUESTIONABLE. BUT IT DID MARK PROGRESS TOWARD EASIER, BETTER HOME LAUNDERING. TODAY, A HOUSEWIFE USING THE NEW TIMELINE* AUTOMATIC WASHER NEED ONLY LOAD IT AND FORGET IT. THIS MACHINE, MADE BY B-W'S NORGE EVEN ADDS A RINSE WATER SOFTENER AUTOMATICALLY. ITS SCIENTIFIC WASHING ACTION GETS OUT DIRT, YET WON'T HURT DELICATE FABRICS.

* Reg. U.S. Pat. Off.

TO COOL EMPIRE STATE BLDG.-- 100 MILLION GLASSES OF ICE WATER DAILY!

THE WORLD'S TALLEST SKYSCRAPER IS AIR-CONDITIONED BY CIRCULATING CHILLED WATER THROUGH ITS 85 STORIES OF OFFICES. TO DO THIS, SOME 6 MILLION GALLONS OF WATER DAILY MUST BE KEPT COOLED TO 42-DEGREES. THE BIG-VOLUME REFRIGERATION COMPRESSORS NEEDED ARE FROM B-W'S YORK. EACH DAY THEY CAN GIVE COOLING EQUAL TO MORE THAN TEN MILLION POUNDS OF MELTING ICE.

DESIGN IT BETTER... MAKE IT BETTER **BORG-WARNER**®

32

Believe It or Not!

ENGINEERING B-W PRODUCTION T.M.

BORG-WARNER SKILL AND INGENUITY BENEFIT ALMOST EVERY AMERICAN EVERY DAY THROUGH THE AUTOMOTIVE, AVIATION, MARINE, FARM MACHINERY AND HOME EQUIPMENT FIELDS!

19 OUT OF THE 20 MAKES OF CARS CONTAIN ESSENTIAL B-W PARTS. EVERY COMMERCIAL PLANE AND MANY SHIPS HAVE VITAL B-W COMPONENTS. 9 OUT OF 10 FARMS USE B-W EQUIPPED MACHINES. EVERY OIL FIELD USES B-W EQUIPMENT. MILLIONS OF HOMES HAVE B-W BUILDING MATERIALS, EQUIPMENT AND APPLIANCES.

SPRINKLERS OF B-W CYCOLAC "DISAPPEAR" WHEN NOT IN USE.

AMERICANS STILL START 18 FOREST FIRES AN HOUR!

COOPERATION OF AMERICANS HAS HELPED REDUCE FOREST FIRE LOSSES BY TWO THIRDS DURING THE PAST DECADE. YET THE WOODLANDS BURNED LAST YEAR TOTALLED SOME 9,000,000 ACRES. CARELESSNESS ALONE STILL STARTS FOREST FIRES AT THE RATE OF ALMOST 500 A DAY! YOU CAN HELP CUT THIS WASTE JUST BY BEING CAREFUL WITH CIGARETTES AND MATCHES. **OBSERVE FORESTRY RULES!**

THIRSTY ROOTS CAN NOW ORDER "RAIN" THEY NEED!

THE NEWEST LAWN SPRINKLING SYSTEM USES A BURIED MOISTURE "SENSER". WHENEVER ROOTS NEED WATER, IT TURNS ON SPRINKLERS THAT POP UP AND SPRAY. WHEN THE GROUND IS SOAKED, THE SYSTEM SHUTS ITSELF OFF. TO ASSURE DEPENDABLE OPERATION YEAR AFTER YEAR, VITAL PARTS, INCLUDING WATER LINES, FITTINGS, AND SPRINKLERS, ARE MADE OF CYCOLAC* THIS TREMENDOUSLY TOUGH NEW PLASTIC FROM **B-W's MARBON CHEMICAL** WITHSTANDS GRIT, HEAT--EVEN WINTER FREEZING.

JET PILOT HITS PLANES THAT ARE NEVER WHERE HE SEES THEM!

HUMAN EYES ARE TOO SLOW FOR JET-SPEED COMBAT. A PILOT SEES AN ENEMY JET CUTTING IN FRONT OF HIM ONLY AS A PHANTOM-- AN AFTER-IMAGE. ACTUALLY IT IS 88 FEET OR MORE BEYOND. BUT THE NEWEST FIRE-CONTROL SYSTEM "SEES" THE REAL TARGET. IT THEN FLIES HIS PLANE ON A DEAD AIM COURSE BY MEANS OF SENSITIVE CONTROL MECHANISMS FROM **B-W's WESTON HYDRAULICS**. RESPONDING WITH SPLIT-SECOND SPEED TO A STREAM OF ELECTRICAL SIGNALS, THESE MECHANISMS "STEER" THE PLANE UNERRINGLY TO ASSURE A DIRECT HIT WHEN THE WEAPONS FIRE.

1957

Celebrities
Attend Opening
Of New Show At
The Lido In Paris
And Anyone Who's
Anyone Attends

Yves **M**ontand &
Simone **S**ignoret

Michelle **M**organ

Salvador **D**ali

The **D**uke & **D**uchess of **W**indsor

Françoise **S**agan

Maurice **C**hevalier

The new and zesty show scores an instant hit.

GALA BALL FOR VETERANS

The glamour and excitement of New York's social season is enhanced by India's Mrs. Aga Khan who arrives at the swank Waldorf Astoria to preside over a ball to raise funds for the Musician's Emergency Fund for hospitalized vets of the Musician's Union.

Wearing over one million dollars in diamonds, the guest of honor reigns over one of the most glittering social events of the season.

A spanking new 1957 car is the grand prize.

The guest of honor dancing with Prince Oberlinsky.

Anyone who's anyone in blue-blood New York circles would have to be seen on the dance floor on this most elegant occasion.

Queen Elizabeth Visits Paris

Paris is filled with excitement as it anticipates the visit of Queen Elizabeth II.

The first visit by a Royal Monarch in twenty years is jam-packed with ceremonial events. Here the Queen lays a wreath at the Tomb of the Unknown Soldier.

Speaking in French, the Queen makes a toast thanking her host for such a warm and gracious reception.

Queen Elizabeth and Prince Philip are the guests of honor at a state dinner.

Queen Elizabeth Flies To Portugal To End Rumors Of A Royal Rift

Prime Minister Macmillan accompanies Queen Elizabeth as she gets ready to fly to Portugal to reunite with Prince Philip.

A crowd of the Queen's loyal subjects gather to wish her bon voyage.

The Duke of Edinburgh has been on a round-the-world trip and has been separated from the Queen for four months, the longest separation in their 10-year marriage, giving rise to speculations of domestic difficulties.

Queen Elizabeth and Prince Philip are greeted at the White House by First Lady Mamie Eisenhower.

Queen Elizabeth &

Prince Philip and Mamie.

A water display in New York Harbor for the Queen's enjoyment.

A smiling Queen watches the waterworks.

Wall Street rolls out its carpet for the young Monarch with an extra special ticker tape parade.

Prince Philip
Visit
America

Wall Streeters line the sidewalks to catch a glimpse of her royal face.

1957

In The Fabled Kingdom Of Monaco A New Princess Has Arrived.

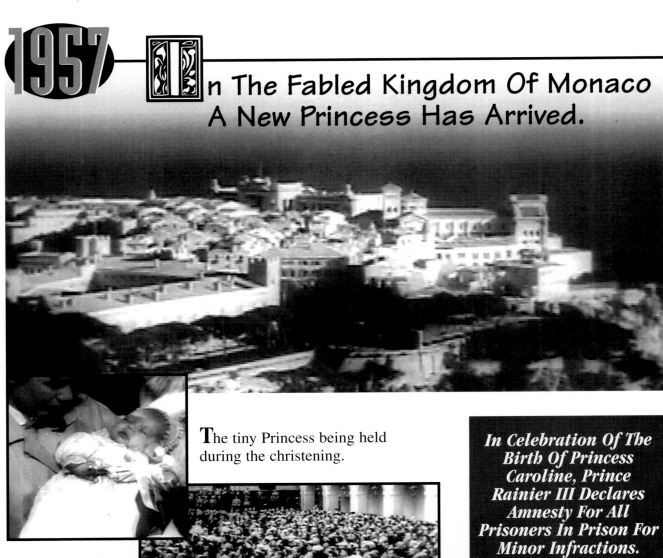

The tiny Princess being held during the christening.

Crowds gather to celebrate the christening of Princess Caroline.

In Celebration Of The Birth Of Princess Caroline, Prince Rainier III Declares Amnesty For All Prisoners In Prison For Minor Infractions.

❀

In A Bulletin From The Palace, Princess Grace Of Monaco Announces That Contrary To Rumors, Baby Princess Caroline Does Not Suck Her Thumb Or Indeed Any Other Fingers And That She Dislikes Hats And Having Her Picture Taken.

The proud parents emerge from the church holding Caroline for her first public appearance.

With another Royal arrival expected in March, everyone's rooting for a boy.

WHAT A YEAR IT WAS!

Prince Charles Becomes The First British Heir To The Throne To Enter A Preparatory School.

IS THIS ANY WAY TO TREAT A PRINCE?

Prince Charles, Heir To The British Throne, Enters Cheam School Where He Will Share An Unheated Dorm With Seven Boys, Sleep On A Wooden Springless Bed, Get Caned For Misconduct And Be Limited to $.35 A Week Spending Money.

Duke & Duchess Of Windsor Negotiate To Buy Burial Plot At Baltimore's Exclusive Green Mount Cemetery.

Queen Mother Elizabeth, Royal Chancellor Of London University, Bestows Honorary Doctor Of Music Degree Upon Her Daughter, Rock 'N' Roll Devotee, Margaret.

After Reviewing The Royal Phone Bills Which Amounted To $70,000 Annually, Queen Elizabeth Decides To Install Pay Telephones In Buckingham Palace To Cut Down On The High Costs.

Despite Ingrid Bergman's Convincing Performance, After Studying A Mountain Of Evidence Including The Testimony Of Anthropologists Who Compared Her Facial Structure To Photographs Of The Teen-Ager, The 83rd Civil Chamber Of The West Berlin District Court Ruled That Anna Anderson Is Not Anastasia, The Romanov Princess Who Supposedly Was The Only Member Of The Royal Family To Escape Bolshevik's Bullets, And Has No Claims To The Late Russian Czar's Fortune.

1957

Jackie Gleason And His Date Are Asked To Leave Manhattan's Swanky Stork Club Because Of Unruly Behavior.

HOLLYWOOD HOTLINE

Eartha Kitt Dines With Prime Minister Jawaharlal Nehru As Part Of Her Around-The-World Quest For Truth, Meaning And Knowledge.

HEDY LAMARR QUITS HOLLYWOOD IN PROTEST OVER THE NON-DEMANDING ROLES IN WHICH SHE IS CAST.

 Maya Angelou Records An Album Entitled "Miss Calypso" Which Is Released By Liberty Records.

Sal Mineo Tries Career As A Rock 'N' Roll Singer.

Dean Martin And Jerry Lewis Break Up Due To Conflicts.

Snoopy Joins Charlie Brown's Baseball Team.

Abbott & Costello, Broke And Facing Problems With The Internal Revenue Service, Split Up.

Refusing To Acknowledge Sophia Loren And Carlo Ponti's Mexican Marriage By Proxy, The Vatican Attacks The Couple Accusing Them Of Living In Sin And Threatens Excommunication.

Colonel And Veteran Of 20 Combat Bomber Missions Over Germany In World War II, Actor James Stewart Is Nominated For Promotion To Brigadier General.

Marie "The Body" McDonald's Hysterical Claim Of Being Kidnapped, Doped, Raped And Left In The California Desert Thought To Be A Hollywood Stunt.

Elvis Presley Reports To A Memphis Induction Center For Exam.

Unhappy With Graham Sutherland's Portrait Of Her Husband Winston, Lady Churchill Put A Match To It With Winnie Concurring That It Makes Him Look Half-Witted.

Sir Winston Churchill's Eldest Daughter Diana Separates From Her Husband Duncan Sandys After 21 Years Of Marriage.

Harry & Bess Truman Left Independence, Missouri To Visit Their New Grandson, Clifton Truman Daniel, With Baseball Mitt In Hand. When Asked If He Would Like The Baby To Be President Some Day, The Ex-President Replied That "He Wouldn't Wish That On Anyone..."

A.F.L.-C.I.O. United Auto Workers Gets Approval From Harry S. Truman To Purchase His Birthplace In Lamar, Missouri For Conversion To A National Museum.

At Over 89 1/2 Years Old, Rhode Island's Democratic Senator Theodore Francis Green Becomes Oldest Man To Ever Serve In The U.S. Congress.

MAN OF THE YEAR

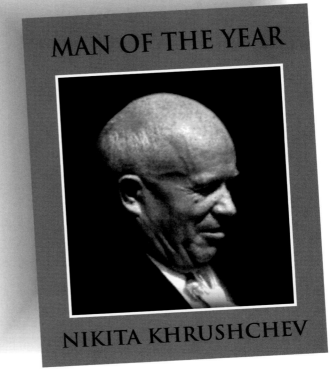

NIKITA KHRUSHCHEV

Ernest Hemingway's
Dog Shot By Cuban Soldiers.

Frank Lloyd Wright
Interviewed On "Mike Wallace Interviews" Show.

MAY YOUR NEXT HOUSE FALL DOWN ABOUT YOUR EARS!
Infuriated That One Of His Structures Known As The Robie House Was Going To Be Torn Down To Build A Dormitory For The Chicago Theological Seminary, 87-Year Old Frank Lloyd Wright Declared That Such Destruction Could Only Take Place In America.

WHAT A YEAR IT WAS!

1957

AMERICA'S RICHEST MEN OR...BUDDY CAN YOU SPARE A MILLION?

Sid W. Richardson	($700 Million)
J. Paul Getty	($700 Million)
Arthur Vining Davis	($450 Million)
Henry Ford II	($400 Million)
Joseph Newton Pew Jr.	($350 Million)
Howard Hughes	($350 Million)
Clint Murchison	($300 Million)
Paul Mellon	($250 Million)
August A. Busch Jr.	($250 Million)
John Davison Rockefeller III	($250 Million)
Robert Winthrop Woodruff	($200 Million)

AMERICA'S RICHEST WOMEN
LADY, CAN YOU SPARE A GIVENCHY?

MRS. HORACE DODGE, Sr.
DORIS DUKE
MRS. ALFRED DuPONT
MRS. EDSEL FORD
MRS. FREDERICK GUEST
MRS. CHAUNCEY McCORMICK
MRS. MERRIWEATHER POST
MRS. C.S. PAYSON
MRS. MARY G. ROEBLING
HELENA RUBINSTEIN

AMERICAN WOMEN PICK THE MOST INTERESTING MEN ALIVE

Sir Winston Churchill

John F. Kennedy

Bishop Fulton J. Sheen

Dag Hammarskjold

Henry Cabot Lodge, Jr.

Major Charles E. Yeager

Leonard Bernstein

Alfred Hitchcock

Paul Anderson

Peter Freuchen

Bobby Morrow

Frank Gifford

Mickey Mantle

Tab Hunter

Tony Trabet

Frank Sinatra

Albert Schweitzer

President Eisenhower

Edward R. Murrow

Toni Sailer

Dr. Harold Taylor

Roger Bannister

Pablo Picasso

Duke Of Edinburgh

Jose Greco

Harry Belafonte

Alfonso De Portago

Arthur Godfrey

Bing Crosby

Elvis Presley

Liberace

WHAT A YEAR IT WAS!

COUPLING

❤ Alan Alda & Arlene Weiss ❤ John Derek & Ursula Andress ❤ John Carradine & Doris Rich ❤ Bing Crosby & Kathryn Grant ❤ Linda Darnell & Merle Roy Robertson ❤ Anthony Franciosa & Shelley Winters ❤ Rex Harrison & Kay Kendall ❤ Howard Hughes & Jean Peters ❤ Jill Ireland & David McCallum ❤ Martin Landau & Barbara Bain ❤ Sophia Loren & Carlo Ponti ❤ Lee Remick & William Colleran ❤ Elizabeth Taylor & Michael Todd ❤ Francois Truffaut & Madeleine Morgenstern ❤ Robert Wagner & Natalie Wood ❤ Henry Fonda & Contessa Afdera Franchetti ❤ Susan Hayward & Floyd Eaton Chalkley ❤ T.S. Eliot & Esme Valerie Fletcher ❤ Lady Iris Mountbatten & Michael N. Bryan ❤ Harry Belafonte & Julie Robinson ❤ Don Larsen & Corrine Audrey Bress ❤ Marlon Brando & Anna Kashfi ❤ Nanette Fabray & Ranald MacDougall ❤ Lee J. Cobb & Mary Hirsch

UNCOUPLING

Elizabeth Taylor & Michael Wilding — Lana Turner & Lex Barker — George Sanders & Zsa Zsa Gabor — David Lean & Ann Todd — Brigitte Bardot & Roger Vadim — Ginger Rogers & Jacques Bergerac — Ingrid Bergman & Roberto Rosselini — Gene Kelly & Betsy Blair — Michael Caine & Patricia Baines — Rex Harrison & Lilli Palmer — Frank Sinatra & Ava Gardner — Harry Belafonte & Frances Marguerite Byrd Belafonte — Judy Holliday & David Oppenheim — Frank Loesser & Mary Alice Loesser — Aly Khan & Rita Hayworth — Jack Webb & Dorothy Towne — Edith Piaf & Jacques Pills

Guess Who's Not Going To Be Bringing Home The Bacon?

An Australian Judge Grants A Woman A Divorce On The Grounds That On Returning Home Early From Her Vacation, She Found Her Husband In Bed With Another Women, Who, Mistaking Her For The Maid, Ordered Bacon And Eggs.

YOU DID WHAT ON YOUR FIRST DATE???
Popo Phillips Celebrates Her First Anniversary As Abby Van Buren, The Fastest Rising Lonelyheart Columnist In The U.S. Syndicated In 80 Papers, She Is Now Ranked Fourth After Dorothy Dix, Mary Haworth and Sister, Ann Landers.

How sugar can help you reduce – and stay there

Why do people find it easier to lose weight than keep it off?

Do you dread starting "another diet"?

Why does overdieting often fail to control overweight?

New facts show how sugar helps you reach your desirable weight, and hold it!

Q. Is it true that more than half the people who lose weight gain it back?

A. Yes, according to a Gallup poll, that is exactly what happens. Often, it is because a person *cuts out* foods to reduce. As soon as he puts these foods back into his meals, and eats the way he used to, the pounds come creeping back.

Q. Does that mean you have to cut out fattening foods all your life?

A. Nutritionists say it is a mistake to think of any single food as "fattening." No one food is fattening in itself when eaten in sensible amounts. There is a simple rule for losing weight, and the same plan can be adapted for *keeping* weight off.

Q. What is the simple rule for losing weight?

A. A leading authority advises this plan: Eat the same foods you are accustomed to, in good variety. Simply go light on the portions. This common-sense plan includes sugar, both for its energy value, and as an aid in cutting down.

Q. How can sugar help you eat less?

A. You may remember when you were small, your mother wouldn't let you have a cookie or piece of candy before a meal because you wouldn't eat all your dinner. Perhaps mother didn't know the scientific reason, but it is a fact that *no other food stems the appetite faster than sugar*. In fact, sugar has been called "The Great Satisfier." If you are trying to cut down on portions, a nibble of something sweet shortly before a meal may keep you from eating far more calories than you need at mealtime.

Q. What happens if you cut down too far?

A. You must remember that carbohydrate foods, such as sugar, are used primarily for energy—the kind of energy your body needs for every action, every heartbeat, every breath. When these foods are trimmed too drastically, nature sends out warning signals to slow down. You have a feeling of tiredness, of brain fag, even irritability.

Q. What if you have to keep going, anyway?

A. Nutritionists have found that an Energy Break helps in mid-morning or afternoon—a piece of candy, or a cookie or a beverage with sugar in it. This is what is meant by the "Scientific Nibble." Sugar is the quickest source of energy there is. *Ounce for ounce, no other food supplies energy so fast, with so few calories.*

Q. Would an artificial sweetener supply energy as fast?

A. No. Artificial sweeteners have no energy value whatsoever. Perhaps even more significant are these findings: *People who gave up sugar and used artificial sweeteners lost no more weight than those who used sugar* . . . the result of a 3-year study of overweight people by one of the nation's leading Universities.

Q. How can I keep my weight down after I reduce?

A. If you start to gain, eat a little less. Again nutritionists say, *don't cut out*. You'll find sugar helpful, not only for supplying energy, but as an appetite appeaser, too. You can live all your life with smaller portions if you feel satisfied and

well, and enjoy the foods that make meals a pleasure.

18 CALORIES!

Surprise you that there are only 18 calories in a level teaspoonful of sugar? (Some people have guessed as high as 600.)

No other food stems your appetite so fast with so few calories

FREE BOOKLET. *Write for your free copy of "The Scientific Nibble."* Contains actual dieting program based on the sensible new approach to weight control.

SUGAR INFORMATION, INC.
New York 5, New York

All statements in this message apply to both cane and beet sugar.

48

The Perfect 10+ Face

The Caricaturists Society Of America Announce The Perfect Composite Female Face:

EYES:	Elizabeth Taylor	(Violet, Limpid)
FOREHEAD:	Kim Novak	(White, Smooth, Pure)
MOUTH:	Anita Ekberg	(Ripe, Sultry, Suggestive)
NOSE:	Teresa Brewer	(Cute, Slightly Turned Up)
HAIR:	Sophia Loren	(Silky, Soft)
CHIN:	Natalie Wood	(Firm, Round & Cute)
NECK:	Barbara Ann Scott	(Slender, Strong)
EYEBROWS:	Maria Callas	(Sulky, Passionate)
EARS:	Helen Stevenson Meyner	(Delicate, Small)

BODY CLINCHING OF A DIFFERENT KIND Former Middleweight Boxing Champion Jake La Motta Is Convicted On Charges Of Aiding And Abetting A 14-Year Old Prostitute Hustle "Johns" In His Miami Bar.

Clare Booth Luce Receives The University Of Notre Dame's Laetare Medal For Her Brilliant Career.

Serving A Life Sentence For Killing His Wife, Dr. Sam Sheppard Is Informed That A Convict And Drug Addict Named Donald Wedler Confessed To The Brutal Crime.

In His Unrelenting Battle Against Smoking, Well Known Surgeon Alton Ochsner Advocates Legal Prohibitions Of Cigarettes If The Number Of Lung Cancer Victims Continues To Increase At The Current High Rate.

10-Year Old Robert Strom Wins Record Sum Of $192,000 On National Television Quiz Program.

PASSINGS

Grace Goodhue Coolidge, Beloved First Lady During Her Husband Calvin's Presidency, Dies At 78.

George "Bugs" Moran, Survivor Of The 1929 Valentine's Day Massacre, Dies At 64 In Fort Leavenworth Federal Prison.

Elliott Ness, Organizer And Leader Of The "Untouchables," A Squad Of Nine Honest Agents Assigned To Nailing Al Capone, Badgering Him Until Undercover Internal Revenue Agents Uncovered Evidence Of Tax Evasion, Dies At 54.

Frank Gannett, Who Built A Newspaper Empire Consisting Of 22 Papers, Four Radio Stations And Three Television Stations, Dies In New York At Age 81.

Notorious Murder Inc. Figure Albert Anastasia Is Gunned Down In A New York Barber Shop At 55.

Herbert Pulitzer, Only Surviving Son Of The Late Great Editor Joseph Pulitzer, Dies At 61.

WHAT A YEAR IT WAS!

King-Size Birthday Card: ▶
Opens to a foot and a half of wishes for the biggest birthday ever. A Norcross exclusive, in your dealer's special rack. Price $1.00.   Shown is #100HB993.

◀ **Queen-Size Convalescent Card:**
Stands 12 inches high, for an extra measure of "Get Well" cheer. Look for this Norcross extra in its special rack at your dealer's. Price 50 cents. Shown is #50CN700.

There's a message here for someone you know

There's someone you can make happier today by saying "I'm thinking of you." Your thoughts, warmly and sincerely expressed in Norcross greeting cards will make you dearer to those you care about.

Whether you say "Happy Birthday," "Get Well," "Congratulations," or just "Hello," Norcross greeting cards say what you want to say. See the beautiful selection —from 5¢ to $1.00—displayed at your Norcross dealer's. You'll be delighted with the many wishes, said in so many pleasing ways.

NORCROSS **N** GREETING CARDS
Say the things you want to say

©NORCROSS, INC.

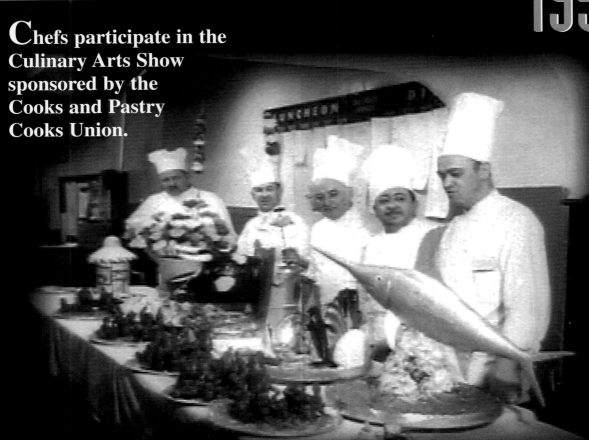

Chefs participate in the Culinary Arts Show sponsored by the Cooks and Pastry Cooks Union.

HUMAN INTEREST

These most talented chefs show off their totally edible creations.

1957

PLATYPUSES COME TO AMERICA

New York's Bronx Zoo built a special tank to house three Platypuses sent from Australia – the only ones in captivity in the U.S.

A happy zookeeper gives a smiling welcome as he holds one of these odd little fellows.

In any case, these kids are having a great time with a new-found playmate.

The Platypus is a mammal that lays eggs, swims like a fish, looks like a beaver and is a puzzlement to scientists.

High school students in Houston, Texas practice Super Yo-Yo or Cheer-E-O, a revised form of yo-yo brought down from Canada by nine Canadian champs.

The Canadian visitors demonstrate the technical difference between the two pastimes.

Experts say that Cheer-E-O with its smoother axle and better balance is a top notch sporting device.

TEXAS YO-YO CRAZE

Claiming an endless array of tricks, the experts demonstrate some of the most popular ones including "The Magic Twirl."

"Cheer-E-O!"

Heroic efforts of neighbors, firemen and volunteers achieve a miracle and after a little more than a day Bennie is freed.

Little Bennie Hooper is trapped at the bottom of a 20-foot well and rescuers begin the task of digging him out.

BOY RESCUED FROM WELL

Bennie's anxious mother.

With the resiliency of youth, Bennie comes through his ordeal with very little injury.

WHAT A YEAR IT WAS!

Three Air Force Stratofortresses Complete 45-Hour World Flight At Average Speed Of 500 M.P.H.

Celebrating Lindbergh's Historic Flight, The Spirit Of St. Louis II Flies The Atlantic In 6.7 Hours.

Commercial Air Service Begins Between Tokyo And Copenhagen, Flying Over The North Pole.

The Longest Single-Engine Jet Non-Stop Flight From London To Los Angeles Is Flown By Three U.S. Air Force Pilots.

U.S. Navy Jet Sets New Speed Record Of 3 Hours, 22 Minutes, 50.05 Seconds In Cross-Country Flight From Los Angeles To New York.

The United States Air Force Celebrates Its 50th Birthday.

Major John Glenn Sets New Transcontinental Record In A Navy BV-1P Voight Crusader – 3 Hours, 23 Minutes, 8.4 Seconds.

Civil Defense Officials Predict 2,339,012 Deaths In The Event Of A Nuclear Attack On New York.

Levittown, Long Island Is Thriving Community After First Ten Years Since Its Construction.

Under Heavy Police Guard, First Negro* Family Moves Into The White Suburban Community Of Levittown, New York.

*Negro was the commonly used term in 1957.

New York's Madison Square Garden Is The Site Of Billy Graham's Opening Evangelist Crusade.

100,000 Devotees Pack Yankee Stadium To Hear Billy Graham's Sermon.

Pope Pius Gives Permission To Take Pain Pills.

Federal Trade Commission Cracks Down On False Claims On Arthritis Pain Ointments.

Mayflower II, Replica Of The Original Ship, Sails From England To Plymouth, Mass. In 53 Days.

Remains Of Captain Bligh's Bounty Found Off Pitcairn Isle.

1957

AND NOW FOR SOME QUALITY REPORTING...

"New York Evening Enquirer" Renamed "National Enquirer."

Colliers Magazine And Woman's Home Companion Cease Publishing.

SO MUCH FOR ROCK HUDSON & JOHN WAYNE

Oxford University's Union Society Votes In Favor Of A Motion To Resist The Influence Of American Culture On Their Way Of Life.

Egyptian-Controlled Suez Canal Extracts First Toll From British Ship.

Professor Reuben Hill Of The Institute Of Research In Social Sciences At The University Of North Carolina Claims That Despite The Growing Divorce Rate And Increased Juvenile Delinquency, The American Family Is Not Breaking Up Because The Quality Of Interpersonal Skills Has Vastly Improved.

Los Angeles Revises Its Building Code Allowing Construction Of High-Rise Buildings Using Earthquake Stress Engineering.

According To A Chicago Psychologist, Parents Can Keep Their Children From Developing Anti-Social Behavior By Whispering Loving Words In Their Ears As They Sleep.

Juvenile Delinquency Reaches Epidemic Proportions Around The World.

Major Crime In U.S. Rises By 7.5% According To Director Of The F.B.I., J. Edgar Hoover.

Harry S. Truman Library Opens In Independence, Missouri.

U.S. Flag Flies For The First Time On Wilkes Land, Antarctica.

A 2,400 Mile Telephone Cable Linking California And Hawaii Is Placed In Operation.

Construction Of Entrance Channels And Jetties Begins In Marina del Rey, California.

I BET MY CAR'S BIGGER THAN YOUR CAR.

San Francisco State College Semantics Expert Dr. S. I. Hayakawa Calls New Cars Symbols Of The Male Sex.

ACCORDING TO METROPOLITAN LIFE INSURANCE COMPANY AMERICAN FAMILIES ARE GETTING BIGGER WITH COUPLES NOW HAVING A THIRD OR FOURTH CHILD.

In 58% Of American Families, Wives Either Share Or Have A Dominant Role In Handling The Family Finances.

IF I WAS A RICH MAN...

Four Out Of Five American Men Would Continue To Work Even If They Inherited A Large Sum Of Money.

- THE AVERAGE CAR GENERATES ENOUGH HEAT IN NORMAL CITY DRIVING SPEEDS TO MAINTAIN A TEMPERATURE IN THE WINTER OF 70 DEGREES IN A 24-ROOM HOUSE.

- DETROIT PHYSICIAN DR. ALBERT D. RUEDEMANN, JR. RECOMMENDS THAT CARS BE EQUIPPED WITH FRONT SEAT HEADRESTS TO PREVENT NECK INJURIES IF CAR IS REAR ENDED.

The 6-Lane Major Deegan Expressway Opens In New York.

So, as I was saying to me...well me, what do you want for dinner...Chinese or Italian?

According To A Visiting Professor Of Psychology At The University Of California, The Measure Of Human Intelligence May Be Our Ability To Talk To Ourselves.

WHAT A YEAR IT WAS!

1957

RIKERS ISLAND

27 Prisoners In Rikers Island Penitentiary Receive Reduced Sentences For Heroic Efforts In Rescuing Victims Of An Airplane Crash During A Blinding Snowstorm.

Secretary Of The Interior Fred A. Seaton Designates 9,000,000 Acres Of Land In Northeast Portion Of Alaska As A Preserve For Scientific Wildlife Studies And Recreation.

59 Nations Participate In The U.S. Trade Fair In New York.

STRIKES

36-Day Tugboat Strike Hits New York Harbor.

Six Major Boston Newspapers Go On Strike.

◆ The Supreme Court Rules That First Amendment Protection Does Not Extend To Obscene Material.

◆ A New York Judge Releases Allen Ginsberg's "Howl" Seized By The Police As Obscene Material.

THE POPE REDUCES TO THREE HOURS THE FASTING TIME BEFORE RECEIVING HOLY COMMUNION.

KENYA GETS ITS FIRST AFRICAN ROMAN CATHOLIC BISHOP.

Buddhist Pilgrims Converge On Katmandu, Nepal To Celebrate The 2,500th Anniversary Of The Death Of Buddha.

SAY "I DO" OR DIE... SOONER THAN LATER

Statisticians Of The Metropolitan Life Insurance Company Report That Married Men Live Longer With Death Rate For Single Men 50% Higher Before Age 45. The Difference In Mortality Is Not As Dramatic Between Married And Single Women, However.

PASS THE BUTTER... I MEAN PASS THE MARGARINE

MARGARINE EXCEEDS BUTTER FOR THE FIRST TIME IN PER CAPITA CONSUMPTION.

THE LADY IS NOT FOR BURNING

The 1692 Witchcraft Convictions Of Six Salem Women Is Reversed By The Governor Of Massachusetts.

They Don't Do Windows

Heirs To William Randolph Hearst's 120-Acre Unmanageable San Simeon Estate, A Repository For What Might Be Described As An Art Collection Bordering On Maniacal Megalomania, Decide To Turn It Over To The State Of California With The Proviso It Be Declared A Historic Monument And Memorial To Hearst And His Mother Phoebe.

U.S. Postmaster Halts Saturday Mail Delivery Until President Eisenhower Signs Bill Providing An Additional $41,000,000 Appropriation.

The Postmaster General Establishes The Citizens' Stamp Advisory Committee To Evaluate The Merits Of New Stamp Proposals.

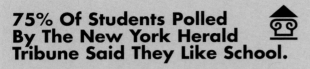

A Visiting Beekeeper At The Rio Claro Apiary In Africa Accidentally Releases 26 Colonies Headed By Extremely Aggressive African Queens.

75% Of Students Polled By The New York Herald Tribune Said They Like School.

ANNUAL COLLEGE COSTS

Public College . . . $1,500 Tuition & Living Expenses
Private . . . . $2,000 Tuition & Living Expenses

YALE UNIVERSITY RAISES ITS UNDERGRADUATE TUITION TO $2,000, THE THIRD INCREASE SINCE WORLD WAR II.

WHAT A YEAR IT WAS!

WE WON'T DO WINDOWS, DISHES, MAKE BEDS, VACUUM OR ANYTHING ELSE FOR THAT MATTER

While 8 Out Of 10 Adolescent American Girls Want To Grow Up And Be Like Their Mothers, They Definitely Do Not Want To Do Housework And While 94% Of Young Girls Want To Get Married, Only 3% Would Consider Being Full-Time Housewives.

Despite The Decline In The Number Of Fully Qualified Geishas, The Girls Are Earning More Money Than Ever Averaging $200 Per Month.

1957

14,000 Negroes* And Whites Gather At Washington, D.C.'s Lincoln Memorial On A Prayer Pilgrimage For Freedom Marking The Third Anniversary Of The Supreme Court's Desegregation Decision.

*Negro was the commonly used word in 1957.

"Gimme A Double Malted On The Rocks…With A Pretzel Stick"

According To A Yale Center Of Alcohol Studies Report Published In The Journal Of The American Medical Association, Alcoholism Is Virtually Unknown Among Orthodox Jews Due To The Symbolic And Sacred Character Of The Use Of Alcohol. The Orthodox Jew Experiencing Emotional Problems Would Be More Apt To Work Excessively, Gamble Or Seek Another Outlet.

HOW DO I HATE THEE, LET ME COUNT THE WAYS…

Researchers At The University Of California, Los Angeles, Come Up With The Most Common Reasons For Marital Failure:

(1) Adolescent Behavior (2) Unconscious Anti-Marriage Feelings (3) Egocentric (4) Homosexual Tendency Or Male Passivity (5) Sexual Dissatisfaction & Projection (6) Rebellion Against Femininity (7) Flight Into Rejection

COPY THE CAT

President Of The American Veterinary Radiology Society States That More And More Dogs Are Developing Ulcers Due To The Pressure Of Urban Living – Traffic, The Barking Dog Next Door, Rough Handling By Children. The Solution: Copy The Behavior Of Cats Who Are Much More Relaxed And Don't Get Themselves Upset Over Little Things.

NEW WORDS &

Asian Influenza
A Different Strain
Of Type A.

**Crane
Helicopter**
A Helicopter
Equipped
With A Crane
For Heavy
Lifting.

**Curtain-
Wall
School**
A School
Made Of
Movable
Walls.

Blast-Down
A Rocket Ship Landing.

Bombardier
A Bomb-Shaped Vehicle
Mounted On Skies
For Snow Travel.

Borazon
A Synthetic
Diamond-Like
Substance.

Flying Seat
An Ejection Seat
Designed By Lockheed.

Little Europe
The Six European
Nations Comprising The
Common Market.

(France, West Germany,
Italy, Belgium, The
Netherlands And
Luxembourg)

Calypsomania
Addiction To Calypso
Music.

Mailster
A Three-Wheel Scooter
For Mailmen

Meter Maid
A Woman Attached To
The Police Force To Write
Tickets For Parking
Meter Violations.

EXPRESSIONS

Rockabilly
A Combination Of Country And Rock Sounds.

Stratospheric Drip
Fallout.

Subliminal Projection
Advertising Designed To Reach The Unconscious Of The Viewers.

Scuba
Self-Contained Underwater Breathing Apparatus.

Skort
Combination Skirt And Shorts.

Teleprompted
Aided By A Teleprompter.

Total Theatre
A Theatre Piece Which Utilizes All Aspects Of The Performing Arts.

Space Biology
The Study Of Effects Of High Altitude On Humans.

Special
A Spectacular Television Show.

White Sidewall Haircut
A Haircut With Hair Clipped Short On The Sides.

New for Christmas! Twin-Cartridge fountain pen
holds 40% more ink...yet never goes near an ink bottle

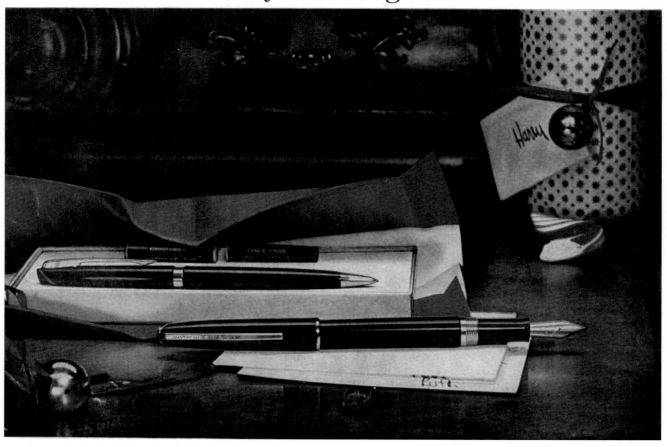

The beautiful new SAFARI pen and pencil are like no other writing set you ever saw before.

The SAFARI pen is a true fountain pen that loads with *two cartridges of liquid ink* . . . never from an ink bottle. It holds 40% more ink than any other fountain pen . . . yet is sleekly modern and slim.

You never run out of ink, either. The second cartridge is a spare . . . always ready right in the pen. And only Esterbrook gives you a choice of 32 points . . . replaceable in seconds at any pen counter.

Two cartridges instead of one — so you always have a spare ink supply. Loading the SAFARI is so easy and clean, too. Just drop two ink cartridges into pen . . . and you're ready to *write.* When one cartridge is used up, replace it . . . and keep the other as your spare ink supply. You can buy economical packs of 6 big cartridges at any pen counter.

And the matching SAFARI pencil is completely unique, too. You feed *two feet of lead* without reloading — simply by pressing its push-top.

People expect Esterbrook's superb new SAFARI pen and pencil set to cost $25.00 or more. Guess again! The sensible price — complete with cartridges — is just $7.75. Pen alone only $3.95.

Esterbrook®
SAFARI*
TWIN-CARTRIDGE FOUNTAIN PEN
only $3.95

Only Esterbrook gives you a choice of 32 points—replaceable in seconds.

student   Signature Stub   bookkeeping   fine writing   shaded writing

*TRADEMARK

Everyday consumer products have been given a new French twist such as this stove in the shape of a snail.

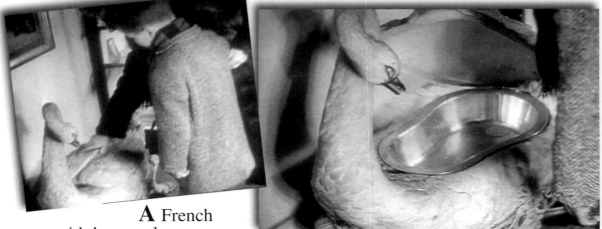

A French woman with her son leans over to remove the cover from what looks like a swan. **G**uess again. It's a wash basin.

And finally, two products that no French household should be without... knives with boots (left), or a cigarette holder with a tiny paper umbrella to keep the smoke out of your eyes.

Illustrated above left to right: #6597 paper-wrapped, #6587 disc, #1207 woodcased.

Corrections are a snap with JOB-MATED ERASERS*

It's natural to make mistakes whether typing, drawing, writing with pencil or ink...on letterheads, carbon tissues, vellums or literally hundreds of kinds of paper.

Now, once and for all, you can forget those human errors. *Change your mind as often as you like.* Because Eberhard Faber

makes a job-mated eraser° for every purpose and every paper. Try one today—at better stores everywhere.

SINCE 1849 **EBERHARD FABER** WILKES-BARRE, PA. TORONTO

Erasers Easily Eliminate Errors

*Mated to the paper type and designed for the erasure job

Trademarks Reg. U. S. Pat. Off.

Pink Pearl "100"... Rubkleen "6002"... Ruby "112"... Star Plastic Cleaner ... Specify choice of eraser on your company letterhead for free sample

AMERICA'S FIRST COMMERCIAL JET TAKES TO THE SKIES

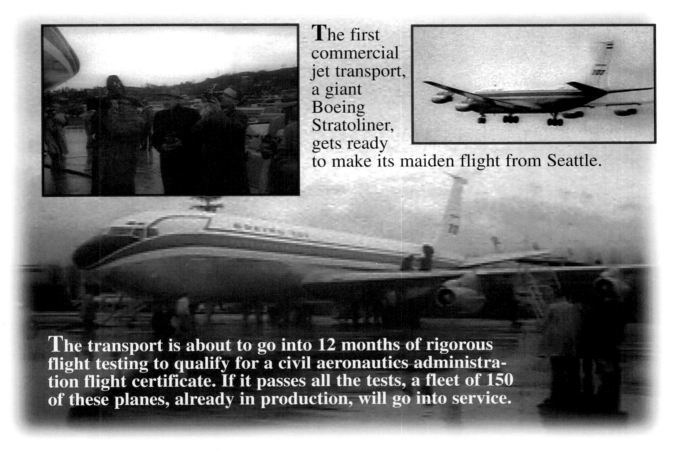

The first commercial jet transport, a giant Boeing Stratoliner, gets ready to make its maiden flight from Seattle.

The transport is about to go into 12 months of rigorous flight testing to qualify for a civil aeronautics administration flight certificate. If it passes all the tests, a fleet of 150 of these planes, already in production, will go into service.

DIGITAL Equipment Corporation Is Founded

Proctor & Gamble Acquires Charmin Paper Mills And Clorox

PASSINGS

Diamond king **SIR ERNEST OPPENHEIMER**, owner of the De Beers Mines and controller of 95% of the world's diamond products, dies at age 77 in Johannesburg.

Automobile pioneer **LOUIS SEMPLE CLARKE**, who built his first car in 1896, dies at age 90.

this was the price that was

Baseball	2.77
Bath Towel	.74
Coca-Cola	.05
Iron, Electric	6.27
Flashlight Battery	.14
Diapers, Fleece	2.69

Aspirin (100 ct.)	$ .49
Baby Powder (4 oz.)	.49
Bath Salts	2.50
Billfold, Ladies	5.00
Blistex Lip Medication	.39
Box Spring	49.50
Candelabra, Sterling Silver	155.00
Candy (Lifesavers)	.05

China, Cup & Saucer Set	$3.50
Cigarette Lighter	.17
Cigar	.10
Clearasil Acne Medication	.69
Clothes Dryer	199.95
Cold Medicine	1.00
Cologne & Dusting Powder Set	3.00
Cooking Pot & Cover, Stainless Steel (2 pcs.)	5.99
Cough Syrup	.39
Curtains & Valance	.97
Dental Cream	.65
Deodorant (Cream)	.43
Electric Shaver	14.95
Ex-Lax Laxative	.79
Eye Shadow Stick	1.00

Eyebrow Pencil, Automatic	$ .79
Eyelash Curler	1.00
Hair Tonic	.49
Home Permanent, Toni	2.29
Lamps, Boudoir	1.47
Lighter Fuel (8 oz.)	.49
Lipstick	1.10
LIFE Magazine	.25
LIFE Magazine, 1-yr subscription	6.75
Make-Up (Liquid)	1.50
Mascara	1.25
Mattress	49.50
Mixed Nuts	2.00
Nail Polish	.75
Pan, Frying (Electric)	22.95
Percolator (Automatic)	16.95
Rain Boots	2.00

1957 Annual Salaries
(Highest In History)

Accountants	$ 9,336.00
Airline Pilots	13,000.00
Financial Executives	11,300.00
Dentists	12,300.00
Lawyers	10,200.00
Motion Picture Performers	25,000.00
Physicians	14,718.00
Psychologists	8,000.00
Surgeons	18,975.00
Teachers (High School & Elementary)	5,000.00
Television Producers	30,000.00
Television Performers	10,000.00
Average Hourly Pay	2.10

Rent-A-Car (per day)	$7.85
Rubber Gloves (Cotton Lined)	1.49
Rugs (Tweed)	1.57
Sandals (Dr. Scholl's)	9.95
Sea Cruise to Europe (3 wks.)	535.00
Shampoo (Dandruff)	1.50
Shaving Blades (pkg. 20)	.73
Shaving Cream	.79

Soap, Bath	$1.50
Tape Recorder	179.95
Television Set (Sylvania)	119.95
Tires, Car (ea.)	16.99
Toaster, Automatic Pop-Up	21.95
Toaster Oven	14.95
Tums	.10
Tweezers	.29
Vaporizer	8.95

GROCERIES

Apples (lb.)	$ .16
Steak, Beef (lb.)	.97
Bread, white (lb.)	.20
Butter (lb.)	.74
Cheese (lb.)	.59
Chicken (lb.)	.45
Coffee (lb.)	1.04
Flour, wheat (lb.)	.10
Lard (lb.)	.33
Milk (qt.)	.29
Bacon (1b.)	.76
Rice (lb.)	.19
Sugar (lb.)	.11
Veal, (lb.)	1.25

WHAT A YEAR IT WAS!

Why buy another <u>*tube*</u> *of tooth paste?*

Ipana®
is here !

Try the new squeeze bottle dentifrice.

Outlasts 3 giant-size tubes!

SAVE UP TO 40¢

Ipana Plus is a real bargain at $1.19 because it gives more brushings than *three* 53¢ tubes!

ANOTHER FINE PRODUCT OF BRISTOL-MYERS

ipana® PLUS DENTIFRICE

ACTUAL SIZE: Fits easily on any bathroom shelf!

Plus

Flows on easily...

...no waste...no mess!

New flowing formula leaves teeth feeling cleaner, whole mouth fresher than tooth paste!*

Just *looking* at it, you know you're going to like it— this wonderful new way to brush your teeth. Once you *use* new Ipana Plus...well, you'll just never go back to your tooth paste tube again!

New Ipana Plus is so much *easier* to use. A gentle squeeze, and just the right amount flows onto your brush. Stop squeezing, it stops flowing. No waste or mess ever. Unbreakable plastic bottle keeps its neat, new look from the very first squeeze to the last.

New flowing formula is ready to go to work quicker than any tooth paste. It penetrates tiny, hidden crevices between teeth. *Most people who tested it—even against their favorite paste—said Ipana Plus left their teeth feeling cleaner, their whole mouth more refreshed. (With kids who tried it, it was love at first taste!)

Start brushing with new Ipana Plus today. Until you do, you'll just never know how clean your teeth and mouth can feel!

WOMEN'S CLOTHES & LINGERIE	
Bra	$ 2.50
Briefs (4)	.97
Dress, Evening	16.50
High Heels	9.95-13.95
Nightgown	6.00
Nylons (pair)	.87
Pajamas (silk)	30.00
Scarves (silk & rayon)	.77
Slip (full)	9.00
Slippers	7.95

MEN'S CLOTHES	
Belt	$ 5.00
Cuff Links (black onyx)	13.50
Hat	5.95
Jacket (nylon)	5.95
Socks	1.00
Thermal T-Shirt	1.50

PAN AMERICAN AIRLINES
See The World On The World-Wide Plan

Typical Round Trips	Minimum Down Payment	20 Monthly Payments
Miami-Havana or Nassau	$ 4	$ 6
Houston-Mexico City	8	6
New York-Bermuda	10	5
West Coast Cities-Hawaii	25	13
Boston-Shannon	37	20
New York-Rome	55	30
Around The World	135	70

LONG DISTANCE RATES ARE LOW
Daytime Station-to-Station Calls

For Example:	First 3 Minutes	Each Added Minute
Augusta, GA. to Charlotte, N.C.	65¢	20¢
Chicago to Indianapolis	70¢	20¢
Baltimore to Boston	$1.10	30¢
Los Angeles to New York	$2.50	65¢

Rates are lower after 6 pm and all day Sunday. Add 10% federal excise tax.

WHAT A YEAR IT WAS!

MACY'S NEW YORK RECORDS $2 MILLION IN SALES IN ONE DAY, THE HIGHEST EVER RECORDED FOR A DEPARTMENT STORE.

Eli Broad And Donald Kaufman Form Building Company Parlaying Their First Investment Of $25,000 Into Sales of $250,000 On The First Week-End Of Business.

J. Willard Marriott, Owner Of Washington D.C.'s Famous Hot Shoppes, Builds One Of The World's Largest Motels, The Twin Bridges Marriott Motor Hotel, On Seven Acres Along The Potomac In Arlington, Virginia.

The Fiat, An Italian Manufactured Automobile, Enters The U.S. Market.

After Three Years And $250 Million In Research And Development, Ford Unveils Its Latest Model—*The Edsel*.

The British Introduce "The Frisky," A Miniature Car With A Gear Shift Similar To A Motorcycle And The Capability Of Getting 90 Miles To A Gallon Of Gas.

The First Toyota Car Arrives In The United States.

Volkswagen Sells 200,000 Beetles.

Only **Ballantine Ale** brews

"*Brewer's Gold*"

into Genuine Golden Ale Flavor!

Enjoy the genuine—

Today's trend to Ballantine light Ale fits right in with the modern taste for the genuine in food and drink. "Brewer's Gold" is a rare, choice hop...one big reason for Ballantine Ale's deep, rich, genuine flavor! Ballantine alone uses its famous true-ale recipe to capture the precious, delicate flavor of "Brewer's Gold". In all the world, no other beverage brewed has such extra excellence brewed into it. No wonder Ballantine is today's favorite ale by 4 to 1.

It's the trend, friend! They all ask for

Ballantine LIGHT Ale !

EUROPEAN COMMON MARKET TREATY SIGNED IN ROME

Rome City Hall is the site where an historic event is about to take place.

Long a dream, the European Common Market takes its first step forward as representatives from six European nations gather to eradicate customs barriers.

German Chancellor Adenauer, one of the chief statesmen at the conference, leads the discussions.

Belgium's representative signs the treaty, the first of several which are expected to unify Western Europe economically within the next 15 years.

With abolition of tariff barriers and the industrial integration of these nations, a new chapter is opened economically uniting former enemies.

"Any cereal starts the day right ... as long as it's Post Bran Flakes"

LIFE IS SWELL WHEN YOU KEEP WELL ... like you do when you enjoy the "keep regular" benefits of Post 40% Bran Flakes. Tastes so good, too—lots of folks eat it for the flavor alone. That's probably why Post is the biggest-selling bran flakes in the world. Try some—see if you don't feel swell yourself!

"ALL POST CEREALS HAPPEN TO BE JUST A LITTLE BIT BETTER"

Post

40% BRAN FLAKES

The Breakfast Foods of General Foods

74

SCIENCE & MEDICINE

International Geophysical Year Opens With Scientists And Technicians Representing 70 Nations That Will Participate In An 18-Month Environmental Study.

U.S. Air Force Major David G. Simons Completes Record Ascent Of 19 Miles In Pressurized Balloon.

First U.S. Nuclear Power Reactor Dedicated By Army Secretary Wilbur Brucker At Ft. Belvoir, Virginia.

First European Particle Accelerator Opens in Geneva.

Micro Computers Made Possible Through New Cryotron Device.

University Of California's Pioneering Nuclear Physicist Ernest Orlando Lawrence Receives $50,000 Prize From Atomic Energy Commission For His Work In Exploring The Atom.

LEADING GERMAN PHYSICISTS ABANDON ALL NUCLEAR-WEAPON RELATED RESEARCH.

Largest Radio Telescope In The World Built At Jodrell Bank, England.

Prehistoric Skull Estimated To Be About 45,000 Years Old Discovered In Cave In Iraq.

WHAT A YEAR IT WAS!

THE HEART OF THE MATTER

Physicians At Philadelphia General Hospital Develop A Tiny Microphone Enabling Scientists To Study Heart Sounds And Murmurs.

New Instrument Called The Cardioscope Allows Inside View Of The Heart.

The Journal Of The American Medical Association Reports That Urban Dwellers Are Safer From Atomic Fall-Out Than Folks Who Live In The Country.

General Electric Develops Borazon, Synthetic Stone With Hardness of A Diamond.

THE FLOWERS THAT BLOOM IN THE SPRING, TRA, LA

(New Varieties)

CLIMBING QUEEN ELIZABETH:
Rose and Pale Pink Double Blossom Climbing Grandiflora.

JUNE BRIDE:
Creamy White Double Flowers With Moderate Fragrance.

GOLD CUP (Coupe d'Or)
Deep Golden Yellow Double Flowers With Moderate Fragrance.

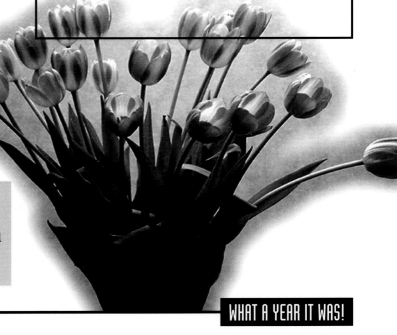

Loyola University Announces Development Of New Powder Food Supplement Which Provides Daily Requirement Of Nutrients.

Physicist Who Helped Develop The Hydrogen Bomb, Edward Teller, Predicts Soviet Scientists Will Be The Best In The World By 1967 Because Of The High Regard In Which Their People Hold Them vs. America Where Scientists Are Thought Of As Squares.

MASSACHUSETTS INSTITUTE OF TECHNOLOGY ANNOUNCES DEVELOPMENT OF A SYNTHETIC PENICILLIN MADE FROM FERMENTED MOLDS.

RCA Builds The World's Largest Electronic Brain For The Army Ordnance Corps. Capable Of Keeping Track Of The Army's Huge Inventory Of Up To 100 Million Facts About Tank And Automotive Spare Parts Throughout The World.

NOBEL PRIZES

MEDICINE & PHYSIOLOGY	PHYSICS	CHEMISTRY
Daniel Bovet (Italy)	Tsung-dao Lee (U.S.) Chen Ning Yang (U.S.)	Sir Alexander R. Todd (Britain)

1957

Space Travel Begins With The Launching Of Laika

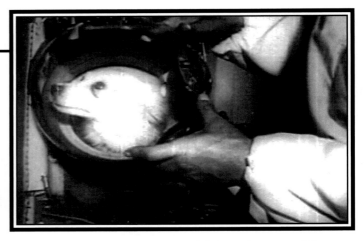

Soviet Scientists Prepare Laika For Her Sputnik Space Launching.

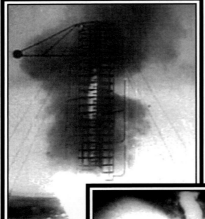

The Rocket Successfully Launched, Laika Is On Her Way To Being The First Space Traveler.

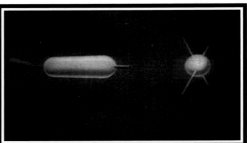

600 Miles In Outer Space, The Half-Ton Satellite Ejects And Orbits The Earth At 18,000 Miles An Hour.

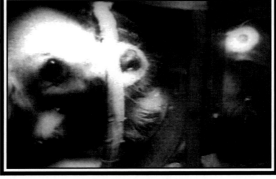

Its Tiny Passenger Is Holding Up Just Great Under The Circumstances.

America Tries To Catch Up With The Soviets.

Shocked At The Launching Of Yet Another Sputnik, America Tries To Catch Up By Trying To Launch A Grapefruit Size Satellite On The Vanguard Rocket.

The Results Are Disastrous As The Rocket Blows Up Two Seconds After Firing From Its Cocoa Beach, Florida Launching Site.

1957

Eisenhower Goes To Paris To Discuss Soviet Space Supremacy.

In The Shadow Of Sputnik, President Eisenhower Goes To Paris To Meet With NATO Leaders To Discuss The Soviet Threat. A Decision Is Reached That Three European Nations Would Be Armed With Intermediate Range Missiles.

President Eisenhower Is Greeted Warmly By The French People.

While In Meetings, Eisenhower Receives Word Of The Successful Launching Of The Atlas Intercontinental Ballistic Missile On a 500-Mile Flight From Cape Canaveral Which Puts America In A Position Of Beginning To Challenge Russia's Space Supremacy.

Watch Spring Implanted In Her Heart Keeps Detroit Woman Alive.

Stanford Medical School Successfully Treats Cancerous Tumors With Their 6-Million Volt Linear Accelerator.

Dr. George Pincus Of The Worcester Institute Of Experimental Biology Develops Pill For Prevention Of Pregnancy In Humans

American, British And Swedish Atomic Scientists Create New Synthetic Element — Nobelium — At The Nobel Institute In Stockholm.

Columbia University Scientists Discover Mountain Range Rising 5,000 Feet Above The Ocean Floor On The Arctic Ice Pack Drifting Toward The North Pole.

Surgeons Find That In Cases Of Uncomplicated Procedures, Patients Recover More Quickly At Home.

Breathing Is More Difficult For Premature Infants Who Are Placed On Their Stomachs Vs. Their Backs.

 American Medical Association Releases Report From American Cancer Society Revealing A Strong Connection Between Cigarette Smoking and Deaths From Lung Cancer.

U.S. Public Health Service Takes Official Anti-Smoking Position Because Of Increasing Evidence Of The Link Between Cigarette Smoking And Lung Cancer.

Poetry Used Successfully As A Healing Aid In Philadelphia State Hospital.

- ❑ American Medical Association To Study Use Of Stimulants By Athletes.

- ❑ Johns Hopkins University Announces Development Of A Vaccine Against Major Common Cold Virus Developed By Winston H. Price.

- ❑ National Association Of Chiropodists Renamed American Podiatry Association.

- ❑ Air Force Veterinarian Harry A. Gorman's All-Metal Device To Replace Hip Joint In Injured Dogs Used On Human Victim Of Rheumatoid Arthritis.

- ❑ Canadian Psychiatrist Discovers New Neurosis: Audiophilia — Excessive Passion For Hi-Fi Sound And Equipment.

- **Sedative Drug Thalidomide Released In Europe And Canada Widely Used To Counter Morning Sickness In Pregnant Women.**

- **Orinase, First Oral Medication For Diabetes, Introduced By Upjohn.**

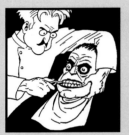

HERE'S SOMETHING TO CHEW ON

According To A Report Released By Seton Hall College, There Is A Definite Link Between Personality And Tooth Decay. A Person Inclined To Have Bad Teeth Has Characteristics Something Like These:

• Independent Self Starters
• Welcomes Responsibility
• Interested In Intellectual Pursuits

According To A Study Conducted By New York's Yeshiva University, Men On Skid Row Are Just As Intelligent As Their Non-Skid Row Counterparts.

Surgeons Enter The Coronary Arteries For The First Time And Remove Fatty Clots That Lead To Heart Attacks.

Medical Investigators Report In The Journal Of The American Medical Association That Eating Red Meat Before A Football Game Does Not Improve A Player's Performance And That Athletes Live Just As Long As Non-Athletes.

Doctors Warn That A Husband Should Never Donate Blood To His Wife Because Of The Danger Of RH-Factor Incompatibility.

OH MY ACHING HEAD

According To A Study On Headaches Released By Louisiana State Hospital, Recurring Headaches Are Most Prevalent In Single Women Under 20 And People Who Are Divorced Or Separated Are More Likely To Have Them Than Their Married Counterparts.

PROFILE OF THE JAYWALKER

- **Potential Suicides**
- **Immature**
- **Personality Deviates**
- **Unconsciously Seeking Danger**
- **Or...Maybe Just In A Hurry To Get Somewhere**

• Hypnosis Found To Be An Effective Anesthetic During An Operation.

• World Health Organization Develops New Technique For Rabies Protection By Giving Small Doses Of Vaccine To Potential Victims.

According To Psychology Professor Dr. Cleo Dawson Women Expect To Be Bossed And Are More Comfortable In That Role Than In The Role Of Being Bossy.

The Nobel Institute In Sweden Develops Blood Test That Could Determine If A Person Is Mentally Ill.

Use Of Forceps To Aid Delivery Thought To Be Responsible For 70% Of Cerebral Palsy Cases — Cesarean Section Seen As A Safer Alternative.

Chronically Depressed Mental Patients Stay That Way Because Of Their Failure To See Anything Happy In Their Future.

The Journal Of The American Medical Association Publishes A Report Stating That Tranquilizers Can Be Injurious To Mental Health And Can Cause Serious Toxic Reactions.

#1 KILLER DISEASE IN THE UNITED STATES: HEART DISEASE.

WELL, I DON'T MIND IF I DO, SWEETIE, FOR MEDICINAL PURPOSES ONLY, OF COURSE!

A Doctor At New York's St. Luke's Hospital Recommends Moderate Use Of Alcohol By Older Persons As An Excellent Way Of Improving The Health Of Their Mind And Body.

THE CHEMICAL COMPOSITION OF TEARS THOUGHT TO BE ABLE TO DETERMINE THE STATE OF A PERSON'S HEALTH.

According To A Study Done At The University Of Wisconsin, Waking Up Tired Morning After Morning Could Indicate That You Are Anxious, Tense, Disinterested, Bored Or Frustrated In Reaching Your Life's Goals And Are Unwilling To Face Your Everyday Problems.

WHAT A YEAR IT WAS! 83

1957

Larger, Frequent Feedings Said To Ward Off Colic In Breast-Fed Babies.

YOU ARE WHAT YOU EAT PERSONALITY PROFILE

Finicky	**Active & Impulsive**
Vegetable Lovers	**Work Alone On Theoretical Problems; Better Planner Than Administrator.**
Salad Lovers	**Outgoing, Social**
Starch Lovers	**Teamworker; Deals With Day To Day Problems; Good Administrator.**

- Two Philadelphia Surgeons Drs. Warren S. Reeses And Turgut N. Hamdi Successfully Implant Artificial Lens Following Cataract Operation.
- Baby Pacifiers Win Favor With Doctors Once Again As A Means Of Preventing Prolonged Thumbsucking And Dental Disfigurement.

BUT HONEY, BE REASONABLE, WHERE AM I GOING TO FIND COAL AT THIS TIME OF NIGHT — HOW ABOUT A PICKLE?

According To A Nutrition Survey Done Of Pregnant Women, 187 Out Of 1,000 Crave Coal, While One Wanted To Eat The Plaster Off Of Her Wall.

PUT AWAY THAT HAMBURGER & FRENCH FRIES

The Trend Toward Giving Solid Foods To Infants Is Wrong According To A Pediatrician Who Believes Solids Should Be Introduced Around The Same Time As The Baby Gets Its First Teeth.

- Darvon Is Introduced As A Pain Killer.
- One-Minute Test For Syphilis Is Developed.

The Average Age Of Lung Cancer Victims Is Around 61.

Smokers Are More Likely To Give Birth Prematurely.

A Study Of 100 Heart Attack Victims Under Age 40 Reveals Stress The Primary Trigger.

A PIECE OF CHOCOLATE CAKE TO KEEP YOU WARM AT NIGHT

Soldiers Fed A Snack Of Between 600 and 1,200 Calories Before Going To Sleep In Sub-Zero Temperatures Woke Up Fewer Times Throughout The Night And Had Less Discomfort From The Cold Than Those Soldiers Who Did Not Have A Snack. Who's Got The Pizza?

PASSINGS

Admiral Richard Byrd, U.S. Explorer, First To Fly Over North And South Poles, Dies At 69.

Joseph William Kennedy, One Of The Discoverers Of Plutonium, The Essential Element Of The Atomic Bomb, Dies At 40.

INVENTIONS & NEW PRODUCTS

POCKET-SIZE RESUSCITATOR DEVELOPED FOR EMERGENCIES.

HAMILTON WATCH COMPANY INTRODUCES FIRST COMMERCIAL ELECTRIC WRISTWATCH.

The Delco Radio Division Of General Motors Develops All-Transistor Car Radio.

Earl Bakken Of Medtronics, Inc., A Minneapolis Based Company, Develops The First External, Battery-Powered Cardiac Pacemaker.

A Copenhagen Yoga Instructor Designs Earth Shoes.

First U.S. Developed Giant Weather Balloon Launched From Japan Carries Equipment To Broadcast Temperature And Pressure Readings.

First Interstate Facsimile Communications Network To Serve Business Is Installed For Reynolds Metals Company.

First Ticket Facsimile System Installed At New York's Pennsylvania Station Allowing Customers To View Available Fares And Seating For Up To 16 Weeks Ahead On Giant Closed-Circuit TV Screens.

Curbside Banking Service Installed In Pontiac, Michigan Bank.

Automatic Air-Traffic Control System Developed By Thomas M. Ferrill, Jr., Of Garden City, New York.

The General Dynamics Corp. Develops First Electronic Telephone.

Johnson's Wax Corp. Introduces Glade, A Home Air Freshener That Destroys Odors Instead Of Just Masking Them.

A Water Repellent For Leather Shoes Is Developed By Knomark Company Of Brooklyn, New York Which Is Said To Protect Shoes From Rain For As Long As Six Months.

The First Portable Icebox Is Invented Using Dry Ice As The Refrigerant.

Magnetic Stud Finder Introduced By Dresden Manufacturing Of Long Beach, California.

Using The Principles Of The Ball Point Pen, The Glu-Pen Corp. Of Hampton, Virginia Introduces The First Glue Pen Which Dispenses A Small Amount Of Glue When Pressure Is Applied To The Point.

Shatterproof Plastic Window Developed By Seiberling Rubber Co. Of Akron Ohio.

Flashing Run-Way Lights Ordered Installed At Airports By C.A.A.

A Miniature Nuclear-Powered Battery With A 5-Year Life Developed Jointly By Elgin National Watch Co. and Walter Kidde Nuclear Laboratories.

B.F. GOODRICH CO. USES ATOMIC ENERGY FOR THE FIRST TIME TO VULCANIZE AUTOMOBILE TIRES.

Hot Dog Fork Designed To Roast Six Hot Dogs At A Time Introduced By Lockey Products, Chicago, Illinois.

Shatterproof, Washable, Chip Proof Lampshades Available For The First Time.

House Of Vision Reports Development Of Unbreakable Lenses For Plastic Eyeglasses That Are Almost As Scratch Proof As Glass.

Pocket-Sized Television Camera Developed By Radio Corporation Of America For Military Use.

The "Legumex," A European Automatic Vegetable Peeler, Makes Its Way Into The American Market.

General Electric Company Goes Into Limited Production With Battery-Operated New Cordless Electric Clock.

Sapolin Paints, Inc., Introduces New Quick-Drying Paint.

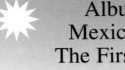 Albuquerque, New Mexico Is The Site Of The First Office Building To Be Successfully Solar-Heated.

First Solar Clock Developed By The General Time Corp., Of New York.

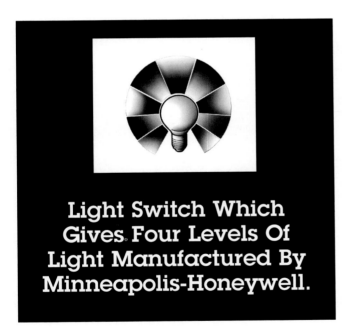

Light Switch Which Gives Four Levels Of Light Manufactured By Minneapolis-Honeywell.

GENERAL ELECTRIC CO. RECEIVES PATENT RIGHTS TO TOASTERS WITH ADJUSTABLE SLOTS TO ACCOMMODATE A GREATER RANGE OF SIZES.

The First Sterling Silver-Tipped Ballpoint Pen Introduced By W.A. Sheaffer Co.

New Curb-Side Telephones With Plastic Hoods To Protect The Equipment Is Being Tested By The Bell Telephone Laboratories.

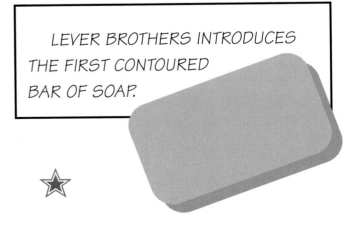

LEVER BROTHERS INTRODUCES THE FIRST CONTOURED BAR OF SOAP.

1957

LEVER BROTHERS ASSIGNED RIGHTS TO PATENT FOR SYNTHETIC PROTEIN COMPOUND MADE FROM SOYBEANS OR PEANUTS FOR USE IN MEATLESS FOOD PRODUCTS SUCH AS HAMBURGERS AND LUNCHEON MEAT.

THE NEW "GENIE-LIFT-A-DOR," A RADIO-CONTROLLED GARAGE DOOR OPENER, IS DEVELOPED BY THE ALLIANCE MANUFACTURING COMPANY IN ALLIANCE, OHIO.

RALSTON PURINA INTRODUCES PURINA DOG CHOW.

THE "AEROCAR," AN AUTOMOBILE WITH COLLAPSIBLE WINGS THAT TURN INTO A 2-PASSENGER PLANE WITH A CRUISING SPEED OF 100 M.P.H. IS DEVELOPED BY AN AMERICAN MANUFACTURER.

Zenith Radio Corp. Develops Streamlined Antenna The Size Of A Box Of Kitchen Matches.

Manhattan's Bohn Duplicator Corp. Develops A 6-Lb. Calculator That Adds, Subtracts, Divides And Multiplies Up To Ten Digits Which Will Sell For $125.

Brooklyn Businessman Benjamin Eisendstadt Develops Sweet 'N'Low With His Son Marty, The Chemist.

Hoover Develops A Spin Dryer For Home Use.

The Frisbee And Hula Hoop Introduced By Wham-O-Manufacturing.

WHAT A YEAR IT WAS!

ENTERTAINMENT

Celebrities Attend The Premiere
In New York Of "The Great Man"
Starring Jose Ferrer

WORLD PREMIERE TUESDAY JANUARY1ST
JOSE FERRER n "THE GREAT MAN"

Opera star ROBERT MERRILL and his wife attend the premiere.

A smiling SAMMY DAVIS, JR. attends festivities alone.

AL MORGAN, author of the best selling novel on which the movie is based, attends the premiere with VICKY DUGAN.

Pals ROBERT ALDA (right), STUBBY KAYE (center) and BILLY GOLDBERG attend this festive event.

"Battle Hymn" Premieres In Colonel Dean Hess' Hometown With Two Days Of Festivities

Marietta, Ohio stages the greatest civic celebration in its history to welcome Colonel Dean Hess and the premiere of his dramatic film biography, "Battle Hymn."

A lavish banquet is given honoring the Colonel.

Festivities continue for two days including this parade honoring all those associated with the film.

Rock Hudson, who plays the Colonel in the film, makes his way through a most enthusiastic crowd.

Rock Hudson, pictured with Dan Duryea.

WHAT A YEAR IT WAS!

The parson who became an ace airman saved thousands of Korean orphans from capture by the reds.

Celebrating Founder's Day, Marietta College bestows an honorary degree on Rock Hudson.

The festivities culminate with the premiere with the biggest crowd ever gathering outside the theatre.

Rock Hudson, Colonel Hess and a City Father smile at the crowd as they get ready to enter the theatre.

WHAT A YEAR IT WAS!

▶▶▶ Exciting gifts – right out of Bell & Howell ELECTRIC EYE cameras!

Electric Eye automatic 8mm. The Electric Eye does all the work. You can shoot action the second you see it (there's nothing to adjust) . . . get good color movies whether you shoot in sun, shade or glare! 290-EE with f/1.9 lens, $169.95.

Electric Eye automatic 16mm. World's first Electric Eye camera. Automatically insures correct exposure of every single foot of film. Magazine-loaded . . . 5 shooting speeds, including slow motion. 200-EE with f/1.9 lens, $329.95.

With this unique Electric Eye these new cameras <u>set their own lenses</u> instantly, continuously— and so accurately that every foot of film is <u>correctly exposed</u>.

Most exciting news in photography! New Bell & Howell Electric Eye cameras are so automatic, even a beginner gets perfect exposures on first try. The Electric Eye does all the work, and it's more accurate than human judgment. You can shoot in shade one moment, in glare the next—without adjusting. Electric Eye ends disappointment over too-light and too-dark scenes!

today's headlines

 Sun Dial simplicity. Just set the dial . . . sight . . . shoot! Styled for family use — and family budgets. On the left: 220 *Wilshire.* Low price includes sharp f/2.5 lens and giant viewfinder. One winding lasts six average scenes. Only $39.95. On the right: new 252-TA *Monterey* turret camera. Has three fast f/1.9 lenses including wide-angle and telephoto. Only $99.95.

8mm movie projector gives big pictures in small rooms. Special f/1.5 Filmovara lens does it. Reverse and still-picture projection, 500-watt lamp. 253-RY *Monterey Deluxe,* $114.95. Other *Monterey* models from $69.95.

16mm movie projector with variable speed control. Slow down the action or speed it up! Run film backwards or stop on a frame! 750-watt concentrated filament lamp. 2" Super Proval lens. 173 *Diplomat,* $299.95.

Electric Eye automatic 16mm threads itself. Electric Eye makes movie-taking as easy as pointing your finger. Spool-loaded . . . 5 shooting speeds. 240-EE with f/1.9 lens, $329.95.

Make someone's Christmas *extra*-special! On this page you'll find something to gladden the heart of any photographer, rank amateur or near-professional. For here are today's most automatic cameras and projectors — with the name "Bell & Howell" on the package to prove it.

See your photo dealer today or write for free illustrated literature. Bell & Howell, Department L-10, Chicago 45, Illinois. In Canada, 88 Industry St., Toronto.

New 35mm slide projector. Has bright 300-watt lamp, powerful cooling fan, semi-automatic changer. *Headliner* 706, $62.50. With automatic electric changer, $86.00. Other slide projectors from $39.95.

Completely automatic slide projector. Shows slides by itself. Viewing cycle can be pre-set. You can hold or change slides from your chair — remote control! *Robomatic* complete with carrying case, $149.50.

 Bell & Howell...finer products through imagination

93

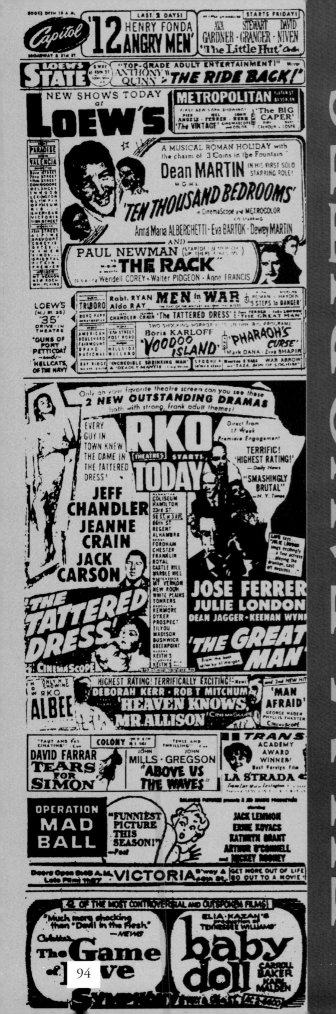

FILM FAVORITES

A Face In The Crowd

A Hatful Of Rain

A King In New York

An Affair To Remember

Aparajito

Attack Of The Crab Monsters

Battle Hymn

Bonjour Tristesse

Desk Set

Delicate Balance

Edge Of The City

Enemy Below

FUNNY FACE

Gunfight At The O.K. Corral

Heaven Knows, Mr. Allison

I WAS A TEENAGE WEREWOLF

Island In The Sun

Jailhouse Rock

Les Girls

Love In The Afternoon

MAN OF A THOUSAND FACES

MAN ON FIRE

Old Yeller

Pal Joey

Paths Of Glory

Peyton Place

Raintree County

SAINT JOAN

Sayonara

Silk Stockings

Something Of Value

THE SWEET SMELL OF SUCCESS

Tammy And The Bachelor

The Bridge On The River Kwai

The Delicate Delinquent

The Helen Morgan Story
The Incredible Shrinking Man
The James Dean Story
The Kettles On Old MacDonald's Farm
The Pajama Game
The Prince And The Showgirl
The Red Balloon
The Seventh Seal
The Spirit Of St. Louis
The Sun Also Rises
Throne Of Blood

The Tin Star
The Wrong Man
THIS COULD BE THE NIGHT
THREE BRAVE MEN
THE THREE FACES OF EVE
Twelve Angry Men
Wild Strawberries
Will Success Spoil Rock Hunter?
Witness For The Prosecution

The Oscar Awards For 1957

(For 1956 Films)

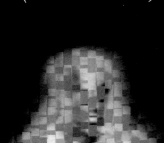

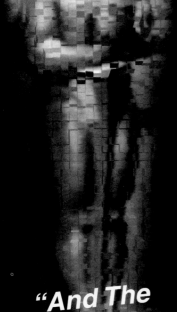

"And The Winner Is..."

1957

Yul Brynner

BEST PICTURE
Around The World In 80 Days

BEST ACTOR
YUL BRYNNER,
The King And I

BEST ACTRESS
INGRID BERGMAN,
Anastasia

BEST DIRECTOR
GEORGE STEVENS,
Giant

BEST SUPPORTING ACTOR
ANTHONY QUINN,
Lust For Life

BEST SUPPORTING ACTRESS
DOROTHY MALONE,
Written On The Wind

1957 Favorites *(Oscars Presented In 1958)*

BEST PICTURE
The Bridge On The River Kwai

BEST ACTOR
ALEC GUINNESS,
The Bridge On The River Kwai

BEST ACTRESS
JOANNE WOODWARD, *The Three Faces Of Eve*

BEST DIRECTOR
DAVID LEAN, *The Bridge On The River Kwai*

BEST SUPPORTING ACTOR
RED BUTTONS, *Sayonara*

BEST SUPPORTING ACTRESS
MIYOSHI UMEKI, *Sayonara*

Fans gather outside the Pantages Theatre to watch their favorite movie stars arrive.

Beaming Robert Stack nominated as Best Supporting Actor for his performance in "Written On The Wind."

A special ovation greets Janet Gaynor who was the first to receive the Best Actress award.

Anthony Quinn receives his second Oscar nomination for his performance in "Lust For Life."

The theatre is jammed with a dazzling array of personalities.

Jack Lemmon presents the Best Supporting Actress award to Dorothy Malone for her role in "Written On The Wind."

An overjoyed Miss Malone makes her acceptance speech.

Yul Brynner receives his Oscar from Anna Magnani for the Best Actor for his performance in "The King And I."

In Ingrid Bergman's absence, Cary Grant accepts the Best Actress award for her performance in "Anastasia."

Mitzi Gaynor presents the Best Picture award to Mike Todd for his "Around The World In 80 Days."

TOP BOX OFFICE STARS

Rock Hudson
John Wayne
Pat Boone
Elvis Presley
Frank Sinatra
Gary Cooper
William Holden
James Stewart
Jerry Lewis
Yul Brynner

John Wayne

Carroll Baker

HOLLYWOOD NEWCOMERS

Carroll Baker
Anita Ekberg
Martha Hyer
John Kerr
Sophia Loren
Jayne Mansfield
Don Murray
Paul Newman
Anthony Perkins
Elvis Presley

Paul Newman

Anthony Perkins

☆ **W**ell-Scrubbed Singer Pat Boone Makes Screen Debut With Shirley Jones.

☆ **50%** Of The Nation's Teenagers See At Least One Movie A Week.

☆ **1,200** Movie Theatres Close As Audiences Turn To Other Sources Of Entertainment— Television Seen As Major Factor.

☆ Hanna-Barbera Productions Is Created When "Tom & Jerry" Animators Joseph Barbera And William Hanna Join Ranks.

"Island In The Sun" Starring **JAMES MASON, DOROTHY DANDRIDGE, JOAN FONTAINE** *And* **HARRY BELAFONTE** *Is First Film To Depict An Interracial Romance.*

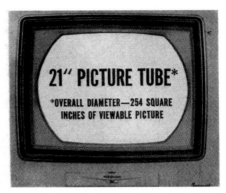

Big as life. Even the lowest priced RCA Victor Big Color set gives a huge 254 square inches of viewable picture—crisp and clear in black-and-white or Color.

All the colors of life. RCA Victor Big Color TV gives Color so natural, so alive—you have to see it to believe it. It's a completely new experience in home entertainment.

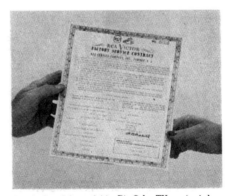

Practical and dependable. Big Color TV service is low-cost—RCA Victor Factory Service Contracts available in most areas, but only to owners of RCA Victor TV.

So simple to tune—even a child can do it. The *Aldrich* (above) in limed oak grained finish (21CS781). $495.

"LIVING COLOR" AT $495 IS NOW BEST TV BUY—IT'S LIKE 2 SETS IN 1

See Color every night — see black-and-white shows, too. RCA Victor Big Color is today's best TV investment!

Here is double-value Color TV at the lowest price in RCA Victor history. Now you and your family will see every program *exactly* as it is broadcast. . . . big Color shows in breath-taking "Living Color"—all regular programs in crisp, clear black-and-white.
New "Color-Quick" tuning—simple, fast, accurate. Turn two knobs and the screen blossoms out in Color. Even a child can tune it.

Your choice of 10 Big Color models—from table model to full-door console in contemporary or traditional styling.
See "Living Color" with your own eyes at your RCA Victor dealer's soon. Ask him about easy budget terms on any Big Color set—your present TV may even cover the down payment!

Manufacturer's nationally advertised VHF list price shown. UHF optional, extra. Prices and specifications subject to change. **At your service:** RCA Victor Factory Service Contracts from $39.95 (90 days).

RCA PIONEERED AND DEVELOPED COMPATIBLE COLOR TV

Like 2 sets in 1 because it's RCA Victor *Compatible* Color. Color shows in Color—all others in black-and-white. This is today's common-sense investment in TV.

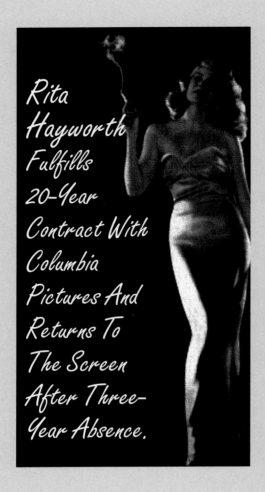

Rita Hayworth Fulfills 20-Year Contract With Columbia Pictures And Returns To The Screen After Three-Year Absence.

FAMOUS BIRTHS

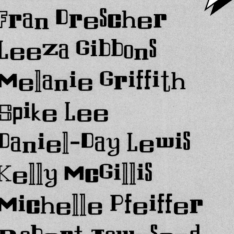

LeVar Burton
Katie Couric
Geena Davis
Fran Drescher
Leeza Gibbons
Melanie Griffith
Spike Lee
Daniel-Day Lewis
Kelly McGillis
Michelle Pfeiffer
Robert Townsend
Mario Van Peebles
Paul Reiser
Rachel Ward
Vanna White

FINAL CURTAIN

Humphrey Bogart dies at 57 leaving a great body of film work including HIGH SIERRA, THE MALTESE FALCON, CASABLANCA, THE CAINE MUTINY and his Academy Award winning performance in THE AFRICAN QUEEN.

Oliver Hardy, considered part of the greatest comedy team in the history of movies, dies at age 65.

Louis B. Mayer, co-founder of MGM, architect of Hollywood's star system and regarded by industry insiders as ruthless and tyrannical, dies at 72.

Pioneer of the "Woman's Film," silent screen star **Norma Talmadge** dies at 60.

Elvis Presley

MUSIC

Harry Belafonte

1957 POPULAR SONGS

A Fine Romance	Ella Fitzgerald & Louis Armstrong
All Shook Up	Elvis Presley
April Love	Pat Boone
A White Sport Coat (And A Pink Carnation)	Marty Robbins
Banana Boat Song (Day O)	Harry Belafonte
Blueberry Hill	Fats Domino
Butterfly	Andy Williams
Bye Bye Love	The Everly Brothers
Chances Are	Johnny Mathis
Diana	Paul Anka
Friendly Persuasion	Pat Boone
Honeycomb	Jimmy Rodgers
Jailhouse Rock	Elvis Presley
Little Darlin'	The Diamonds
Love Letters In The Sand	Pat Boone
Magic Moments	Perry Como
Maria	From "West Side Story"
Marianne	Harry Belafonte
Party Doll	Buddy Knox
Peggy Sue	Buddy Holly
Raunchy	Bill Justis
Rock & Roll Music	Chuck Berry
Round And Round	Perry Como
Seventy-Six Trombones	From "The Music Man"
So Rare	Jimmy Dorsey Orchestra
That'll Be The Day	The Crickets
The Story Of My Life	Marty Robbins
Tammy	Debby Reynolds
Tonight	From "West Side Story"
Too Much	Elvis Presley
Wake Up Little Susie	The Everly Brothers
Whole Lot Of Shakin' Going On	Jerry Lee Lewis
You Send Me	Sam Cooke

FAMOUS BIRTHS

Anita Baker

Gloria Estefan

Vince Gill

Lyle Lovett

George Strait

Donny Osmond

Eddie Van Halen

WHAT A YEAR IT WAS!

Gene Autry

Bing Crosby

Ella Fitzgerald

Popular Singers

(A SAMPLING)

PERRY COMO
BING CROSBY
EDDIE FISHER
PEGGY LEE
DEAN MARTIN
GISELE MACKENZIE
PATTI PAGE
FRANK SINATRA
ELLA FITZGERALD

Frank
Sinatra

Frank Sinatra Sends Telegram To House Judiciary Subcommittee Accusing Columbia's A&R Head Mitch Miller Of Accepting Large Sums Of Money From Writers Whose Songs He Recorded.

New Talent

Paul Anka
Patsy Cline
Sam Cooke
The Crickets
Bobby Darin
The Everly Brothers
Connie Francis
Buddy Holly
Brenda Lee
Jerry Lee Lewis
Johnny Mathis
Ricky Nelson
Conway Twitty
Jackie Wilson

Top Concert Stars

(A SAMPLING)

GENE AUTRY
PAT BOONE
SMILEY BURNETTE
BOB HOPE
RICKY NELSON
ELVIS PRESLEY
JOHNNIE RAY
ROY ROGERS
JIMMY WAKELY

WHAT A YEAR IT WAS!

1957

Downbeat's Top Performers

Miles Davis

JIMMY DORSEY, Jazz Clarinetist And Famed Band Leader Who Scored 23 Hits In The Early 1940's Dies Of Cancer At 53 Just As His Recording Of "So Rare" Reaches # 2 On The Hit Parade.

BENNY GOODMAN
COUNT BASIE
LES BROWN
MODERN JAZZ QUARTET
BARNEY KESSEL
RAY BROWN
ERROL GARNER
JIMMY GUIFFRE
MILES DAVIS
HERBIE MANN
ELLA FITZGERALD
FRANK SINATRA
HI-LO'S

Benny Goodman

♪ 4,000 Rock 'N' Roll Fans Break Through Police Barriers To Greet Bill Haley At London's Waterloo Station.

♪ San Francisco Poets Lawrence Ferlinghetti And Kenneth Patchen Among Poets Fusing Their Poetry With Jazz.

♪ Berry Gordy, Jr. Starts Motown Records.

♪ British Fans Vote Pat Boone The World's Outstanding Singer; Elvis Presley, World's Outstanding Musical Personality; Doris Day, World's Top Female Singer; And The Platters, World's Top Group.

♪ Harry Belafonte's "Mary's Boy Child" One Of The Fastest Selling Singles In Britain.

♪ An Alan Freed Show Starring The Platters, The Teenagers And Buddy Knox Breaks All Attendance Records At New York's Paramount Theatre.

♪ 15-Year Old Canadian Paul Anka Writes "Diana," A Song Dedicated To His Childhood Babysitter.

♪ The Everly Brothers' "Wake Up Little Susie" Banned In Boston.

♪ Buddy Holly And The Crickets Is First White Act To Play Harlem's Apollo Theatre In New York.

♪ A First For Rock 'N' Roll—Sonny James And Tab Hunter Both Reach No. 1 With "Young Love."

♪ West Indian Music Becomes The Rage In The United States.

♪ The Top 40 Format Gains Increasing Popularity With Radio Stations Across The Country.

♪ Hal David And Burt Bacharach Collaborate On Their First Two Big Hits—"Magic Moments" And "The Story Of My Life."

WHAT A YEAR IT WAS!

JOHN LENNON and PAUL MCCARTNEY Meet For The First Time At A Church Garden Party.

♪ Fats Domino Has Three Successive No. 1 Rythmn & Blues Hits—"I'm Walking," "Blueberry Hill" And "Blue Monday."

♪ Pat Boone Performs At President Eisenhower's Inaugural Ball And Signs A $1 Million Television Deal.

♪ Little Richard Shakes Up The Music World When He Announces He Is Giving Up Rock 'N' Roll For Religion.

Teenagers All Over The World Love Elvis And Show Their Enthusiasm By Buying Over Sixteen Million Copies Of His Eight Records And Sending Him Between Forty And Fifty Thousand Letters A Week.

NON-SINGERS SING—
OR WHAT ECHO CHAMBERRRR

Tab Hunter	Young Love
Robert Mitchum	Mama Look-A-Boo-Boo
Jerry Lewis	Rock-A-Bye Your Baby With A Dixie Melody
Anthony Perkins	A Little Love Can Go A Long, Long Way
Grace Kelly	True Love
Fess Parker	Davy Crockett

PLEASE MR. TALLY MAN, TALLY ME ME ROY-AL-TIES

WITH HARRY BELAFONTE'S ALBUM "CALYPSO" BEING ONE OF THE BIGGEST SELLING RECORDS IN RCA VICTOR HISTORY, DO-IT-YOURSELF CALYPSO KITS CONSISTING OF BONGO DRUMS, GOURD AND MARACAS SELL BRISKLY AT $24.50 EACH.

King Of Jazz, Trumpeter LOUIS ARMSTRONG, Angrily Cancels His U.S. Government-Sponsored Tour Of The Soviet Union In Protest Over The Treatment Of Southern Blacks.

WHAT A YEAR IT WAS!

1957

Classical Music

Europe's New Divas

Anita Cerquetti *(Italy)*
Clara Petrella *(Italy)*
Irene Dalis *(U.S.)*
Eugenia Ratti *(Italy)*

PASSINGS

Sibelius

Finnish composer **JEAN SIBELIUS**, who dropped out of law school to pursue music, is dead at 91.

ARTURO TOSCANINI, brilliant Italian conductor who headed La Scala and the Metropolitan Opera, conducting the world premiere of "Pagliacci," "La Boheme" and "Girl Of The Golden West," dies at 89.

BENIAMO GIGLI, one of the most popular operatic tenors of the century, dies at 71.

EZIO PINZA, Metropolitan Opera Basso and Broadway Star, dies at 64.

- Los Angeles Celebrates Igor Stravinsky's 75th Birthday With The Premiere Of "Agon" And "Canticum Sacrum."

- William Walton Composes "Concerto For Cello And Orchestra."

- Carl Orff Composes "Comoedia de Christi Resurrectione."

- Leonard Bernstein Named Musical Director Of The New York Philharmonic.

- Maria Callas Triumphs In Inaugural Concert At New Dallas State Fair Music Hall Opening With An Aria From Mozart's "The Abduction From The Seraglio."

- Dmitry Shostakovich's "Piano Concerto" Performed In Moscow With Maxim Shostakovich The Guest Soloist.

Famed Cellist **Pablo Cassals**, 80, marries his fourth wife, Martita Montañez, a 20-year old student from Puerto Rico.

OPERA PREMIERES

Blood Wedding
Wolfgang Fortner
(Cologne)

Thyl de Flandre
Jacques Chailley
(Brussels)

Assassinio della Cathedrale
Ildebrando Pizetti
(Milan)

The Moon And Sixpence
John Gardener
(London)

The Turn Of The Screw
Benjamin Britten
(Stratford)

The Portrait
Hilding Rosenberg
(Stockholm)

Les Dialogues des Carmélites
Francis Poulenc
(Milan)

Die Harmonie der Welt
Paul Hindemith
(Munich)

Venus In Africa
George Antheil
(Denver)

When better automobiles are built Buick will build them

Solid click on the TROJAN campus

We previewed the B-58 Buick at the University of Southern California — and drew a more enthusiastic turnout than a movie crew on location.

What sent the students the most was that new Miracle Ride, plus Air-Poise Suspension.*

They couldn't get over the way this Buick levels itself, no matter how heavy the load, or where you place it.

They marveled at the way the worst bumps and potholes seemed to disappear beneath the wheels.

And what brought the widest grins of glee was the way this big B-58 sailed up the winding canyon roads without a trace of slew or sway.

When we tallied up the comments, "It's the greatest!" was the mildest.

So — go see what the hubbub's all about, at your Buick dealer's now.

BUICK *Division of* GENERAL MOTORS

Air-Poise Suspension optional at extra cost on all Series.

TRY THE MIRACLE RIDE OF —

THE AIR BORN B-58 BUICK

See TALES OF WELLS FARGO, Monday Nights, NBC-TV and THE PATRICE MUNSEL SHOW, Friday Nights, ABC-TV

111

One Of The Architectural Wonders Of The World, The Sydney Opera House, *Opens Providing A World-Class Cultural Center For Theatre, Opera And Ballet.*

The Israeli Philharmonic, Comprised Predominantly Of Refugees From The Nazis, Moves To New, Permanent Concert Hall In Tel Aviv With Leonard Bernstein Conducting Opening Concert And Isaac Stern Guest Violinist.

Aaron Copland Composes "Piano Fantasy."

Gian Carlo Menotti's Symphonic Poem "Apocalypse" Performed In Pittsburgh.

PULITZER PRIZE FOR MUSIC | Norman Dello Joio *"Meditations On Ecclesiastes"*

Ballet Premieres

Agon
Igor Stravinsky *(Paris)*

The Prince Of The Pagodas
Benjamin Britten

Square Dance
George Balanchine
New York City Ballet

Sebastian
Agnes de Mille
(An experimental piece performed without music, costumes or sets)

I Could Have Danced, Danced, Danced All Night

• **W**ith The Growing Popularity Of American Dance, American Ballet Theatre Sponsors Series Of Experimental Performances In New York.

• **N**ew York City Ballet's Prima Ballerina Maria Tallchief Returns After Brief Illness. Among The New Pieces Premiering Are:
"Pastorale" (Choreographic Debut By Francisco Moncion)
"The Masquers" (Todd Bolender)
"The Unicorn, The Gorgon And The Manticore" (Gian Carlo Menotti, Choreographed By John Butler)

• **T**he Metropolitan Opera House Hosts The Ballet Russe De Monte Carlo In The Debut Of Several New Works Including "Harlequinade," "The Lady And The Unicorn" And "Sombreros."

• **T**he Royal Ballet Visits The Metropolitan Opera House With The Incomparable Margot Fonteyn Dancing In "The Sleeping Beauty," "Swan Lake," "La Péri," "Birthday Offering" And "Petrouchka."

• **T**he Royal Ballet Flies To New York To Perform "Cinderella" On Television With Margot Fonteyn And Michael Somes Dancing The Lead Roles.

• **T**he Renowned Jacob's Pillow Dance Festival Celebrates Its 25th Birthday.

• **A**lwin Nikolais Stages "Runic Canto" And José Limon Produces "Blue Roses" Based On Tennessee Williams' "The Glass Menagerie" At The 10th American Dance Festival Held At Connecticut College.

• **J**osé Limon & Company Begin World Tour Under The Auspices Of The President's International Cultural Program.

PRIME TIME PROGRAMS
(A Sampling)

The George Burns And Gracie Allen Show
The Steve Allen Show
The Eve Arden Show
The Adventures Of Rin Tin Tin
The Adventures Of Robin Hood
The Adventures Of Ozzie & Harriet
Alfred Hitchcock Presents
All-American Football
   Game Of The Week
American Bandstand
Armstrong Circle Theatre/U.S. Steel Hour
Assignment Foreign Legion
Bachelor Father
Red Barber's Corner
The Jack Benny Show
The Polly Bergen Show/Club Oasis
The Pat Boone Chevy Showroom
Bowling Stars
Broken Arrow
Caesar's Hour
Cheyenne
The Californians
Circus Boy
The Nat "King" Cole Show
Colt .45
The Perry Como Show
The Bob Cummings Show
December Bride
Richard Diamond, Private Detective
Disneyland
Dragnet
Father Knows Best
The Eddie Fisher Show/
   George Gobel Show
The Ford Show Starring
   Tennessee Ernie Ford
General Electric Theater
Gillette Cavalcade Of Sports
Arthur Godfrey's Talent Scouts
Gunsmoke
Have Gun Will Travel
I've Got A Secret
I Love Lucy
Kraft Television Theatre
Lassie
Leave It To Beaver
The Life Of Riley

Lucille Ball

The "I Love Lucy" Gang Begins Taping One Hour Specials Called "The Lucy-Desi Comedy Hour."

Desilu Productions Reaches Basic Agreement To Purchase RKO Studios

➤ **The Eisenhower/Nixon Inauguration Is First Videotaped National Broadcast Carried By NBC.**

➤ **"Truth Or Consequences" Becomes The First Videotaped Program.**

➤ **DJ Alan Freed Hosts First Prime-Time Rock Special, The "Rock 'n' Roll Show."**

➤ **"The Jack Paar Show" Makes Its Debut On NBC.**

The Lux Show Starring
   Rosemary Clooney
M Squad
The Gisele MacKenzie Show
Maverick
Perry Mason
The Millionaire
The Patrice Munsel Show
Name That Tune
People Are Funny
Playhouse 90
Dick Powell's Zane Grey Theater
The Price Is Right
The Real McCoys
Restless Gun
Sergeant Preston Of The Yukon
$64,000 Question
The Dinah Shore Chevy Show
The Phil Silvers Show
The Red Skelton Show
The Frank Sinatra Show
The Gale Storm Show
Studio One
Sugarfoot
The Ed Sullivan Show
Tales Of Wells Fargo
The Thin Man
The Danny Thomas Show
This Is Your Life
Tombstone Territory
The 20th Century
The Voice Of Firestone
Mike Wallace Interviews
Wagon Train
The Wednesday Night Fights
Lawrence Welk's Top Tunes And
   New Talent
The Lawrence Welk Show
What's My Line
The Walter Winchell File
The Jane Wyman Show
The Loretta Young Show
Your Hit Parade
You Bet Your Life
Zorro

WHAT A YEAR IT WAS!

Journal Of The American Medical Association Identifies *"Television Legs"* Which Develop Blood Clots From Sitting In Front Of The Television Too Long.

1957

THERE'S NO BUSINESS LIKE MONKEY BUSINESS

After spending almost all of his 4 1/2 years with Dave Garroway on the "Today" show, J. Fred Muggs, the world's most successful chimpanzee, quits to seek greener trees. Amassing a fortune between salary and product endorsements, this rich monkey is the envy of a lot of show biz folks.

- **Dick Clark's "American Bandstand" Goes National On ABC.**
- **The FCC Accepts Applications For Pay-TV.**
- **"Maverick" And "Have Gun Will Travel" Among 10 New Westerns To Make Their Television Debut.**
- **"The Price Is Right" Hosted By Bill Cullen Graduates From Day-Time To Prime Time Television.**
- **Howard Cosell Gets His First Regular Daily Sports Wrap-Up Program.**
- **Kermit The Frog Makes His Debut On Steve Allen's "Tonight Show."**
- **California Studios Produce 60% Of Network Programming Attracting Some Of The Most Talented New York Playwrights And Actors.**
- **Before Admitting To A Congressional Committee That He Is A Fraud, Charles Van Doren, Champion On The "Twenty-One" Quiz Show, Wins $129,000 And Receives 500 Marriage Proposals.**

Singer **Nat "King" Cole**, first black entertainer to host his own network show, quits in disgust after a 13-month run due to the failure of advertising agencies to find a national sponsor.

"LEAVE IT TO BEAVER" MAKES ITS TELEVISION DEBUT.

A report published in Denmark indicates there are more than 50 million TV receivers in use throughout the world with the United States being the number one user at 38 million and Canada number two at two million. Norway and Bulgaria finished last with 500 receivers each.

RADIO

MOST POPULAR TELEVISION PROGRAMS

THE JACK BENNY SHOW
CLIMAX
THE PERRY COMO SHOW
DECEMBER BRIDE
DISNEYLAND
CLIMAX
GUNSMOKE
ARTHUR GODFREY'S
    TALENT SCOUTS
I LOVE LUCY
I'VE GOT A SECRET
MISS AMERICA PAGEANT
PLAYHOUSE 90
THE ED SULLIVAN SHOW
$64,000 QUESTION
UNDERCURRENT
THE LAWRENCE WELK SHOW

Most Popular Evening Radio Programs	Most Popular Daytime Radio Programs
Bob & Ray	Nora Drake
Cavalcade Of Stars	Arthur Godfrey
Cavalcade Of Sports	My True Story
Dragnet	Our Gal Sunday
FBI In Peace And War	Ma Perkins
Gangbusters	Helen Trent
Great Gildersleeve	Young Doctor Malone
Gunsmoke	
Heavyweight Championship Fight	
Allan Jackson And The News	
Monitor	
Official Detective	
People Are Funny	
True Detective Mysteries	

EMMY AWARDS

Best Series: (one hour)	**CAESAR'S HOUR**
Best Series: (half-hour)	**THE PHIL SILVERS SHOW**
Best Actor In A Series:	**ROBERT YOUNG** FATHER KNOWS BEST
Best Actress In A Series:	**LORETTA YOUNG** THE LORETTA YOUNG SHOW
Best Comedian:	**SID CEASAR** CAESAR'S HOUR
Best Comedienne:	**NANETTE FABRAY** CAESAR'S HOUR

"FIBBER McGEE AND MOLLY" LEAVE THE RADIO AIRWAVES ALONG WITH "GANGBUSTERS," "COUNTERSPY" AND "TRUTH OR CONSEQUENCES."

"THE JACK BENNY PROGRAM" IS REPLACED BY "THE STAN FREBERG PROGRAM."

WHAT A YEAR IT WAS!

SYLVANIA'S revolutionary 110° TV tube whittles the bulk from BIG SCREEN portables

The Slimmest Case

New wide-angle tube cuts 7" from former depth. Case is even slimmer than small-screen sets.

The Biggest Screen

New 17" (overall diagonal) tube gives you a larger picture than other 17" tubes. You get a full 150 square inches of viewable picture.

The Clearest Picture

Sylvania's new "S-110" chassis builds added power for extra reach in fringe areas; high voltage assures sharper focus.

SYLVANIA 17" SLIM JIM PORTABLE

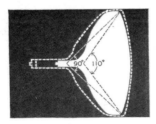

Here is why Slim Jim is slimmer: Because Sylvania has pioneered the development of this new 110° wide-angle picture tube, Sylvania alone can offer you the newest, slimmest, most compact of all 17" portable TV sets.

Here's another TV "first" by Sylvania: the biggest picture in portable TV—in a case so slender it rests anywhere! This family-size set adjusts to its surroundings as easily as tiny-screen sets.

Until now, big-screen portables were deep and bulky because ordinary picture tubes are so deep. But Sylvania engineers have developed a powerful, wide-angle tube that whittles away awkward bulk.

Thanks to Sylvania's exclusive 110° Deflection Picture Tube, Slim Jim is slimmer, lower, lighter—a pleasure to look at.

You can own a Sylvania 17" Slim Jim portable for as little as **$139.95***

*Manufacturer's suggested retail price

SPECIAL INTRODUCTORY OFFER—
with new Sylvania 17" SLIM JIM portables

The exclusive swivel base transforms your Sylvania portable into a console with living-room manners. It swivels the set completely around—a full 360°—angles the picture to your own point of view, makes your favorite chair the best seat in the house.

For a limited time, this handsomely made swivel base is yours for only **$4.88***

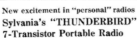

New excitement in "personal" radios
Sylvania's "THUNDERBIRD"
7-Transistor Portable Radio

New, exciting, trim as a sports car, completely tubeless. Sylvania-engineered to pull in distant stations with a clarity new in "personal" radios. Its 7 tiny transistors last far longer than tubes. Room-filling tone—or optional earphones. *Hear it—you'll be amazed!*

Art

JEAN DUBUFFET
"Mirandoliana" painting

HENRY MOORE
"Reclining Figure" sculpture

PABLO PICASSO
"Las Meninas" painting

MARK TOBEY
"Calligraphy In White"
painting

MARK ROTHKO
*"Black Over Reds, Red,
White And Brown"* painting

ADOLPH GOTTLIEB
"Blast I" painting

WILLIAM BAZIOTES
"Red Landscape" painting

ROBERT
RAUSCHENBERG
*"Painting With Red
Letter 'S'"* painting

PHILIP GUSTON
*"The Clock, Painter's
City"* painting

ANDREW WYETH
"Brown Swiss"
painting

RICHARD
DIEBENKORN
*"Girl Looking At
Landscape"* painting

ELLSWORTH KELLY
"New York, New York"
painting

HELEN
FRANKENTHALER
"Jacob's Ladder" painting

SEYMOUR LIPTON
"Pioneer" sculpture

REUBEN NAKIAN
*"The Burning Walls Of
Troy"* sculpture

The Brooklyn Museum Holds A Showing Called "Religious Paintings," Including "Madonna And Child" By Lorenzo Monaco With Other Works By Veneziano, Mantegna, Titian, Tiepolo, Rembrandt, Rubens, Delacroix And Degas.

The Cleveland Museum Of Art Holds An Exhibition Called "The Venetian Tradition" Including Paintings, Drawings And Objects d'Art Dating From The Early 16th Century To The Present Day With Artists Such As Rubens, Piazetti, Watteau, Delacroix, Renoir And Cezanne.

THE LARGEST RARE PRINT EXHIBITION EVER ASSEMBLED IN THE UNITED STATES IS HELD AT THE MINNEAPOLIS INSTITUTE OF THE ARTS WHICH ALSO ARRANGES A LARGE ONE-MAN EXHIBITION OF THE WORK OF CLAUDE MONET IN COOPERATION WITH THE CITY ART MUSEUM OF ST. LOUIS.

The Museum Of Primitive Art Sponsored By Nelson A. Rockefeller Opens In New York.

GOING, GOING, GONE

Gauguin's "Still Life With Apples" Sells For The Highest Price Ever Paid For Modern Art—$346,170 At A Paris Gallery With Renoir's "Mosque In Algiers" And Claude Monet's "Antibes From The Garden Of Salis" Selling For $73,228 And $53,650, Respectively.

Sotheby Gallery Holds London's Biggest Sale Since 1928, Auctioning Off Vincent Van Gogh's "Les Usines á Clichy" At $86,800 And His "Head Of An Angel" For $72,800.

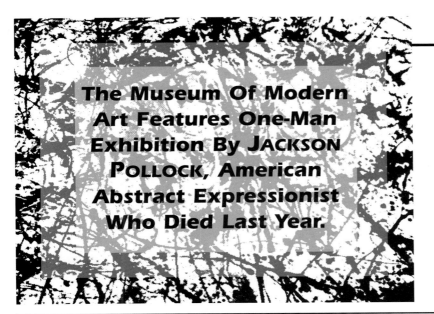

The Museum Of Modern Art Features One-Man Exhibition By JACKSON POLLOCK, American Abstract Expressionist Who Died Last Year.

New York's Museum Of Modern Art And The Art Institute Of Chicago Organize Picasso's 75th Anniversary Exhibition Covering 60 Years Of The Artist's Work Including Pieces From Picasso's Own Collection Including: "The Pipes Of Pan," "Woman Dressing Her Hair," "Paul As Harlequin," "Portrait Of J.R. With Roses" And "Still Life With Chair Caning."

An Exhibition Of The Joseph Pulitzer, Jr. Collection Is Held At The Fogg Museum In Cambridge And The Knoedler Galleries In New York For The Benefit Of Harvard University Including Matisse's "The Bathers" And Picasso's "Woman In Yellow."

ART PRIZES

The Art Institute Of Chicago

Eleanor Coen "Growing City" (painting $1,500)
Robert Anderson "Yesterday, Today And Tomorrow" (collage $1,000)
Richard Hunt "Steel Bloom" (welded sculpture $750)

Pennsylvania Academy Of The Fine Arts

Henry C. Pitz Winner, The Philadelphia Watercolor Club Medal

The 4th Biennale At São Paulo, Brazil

Ben Nicholson Winner, First Prize For Painting (Also received Guggenheim Award of $10,000)

Art Institute Of Chicago's 62nd American Exhibition Of Painting And Sculpture

Seymour Lipton "The Cloak" (welded sculpture, First Prize: $2,000)
James Brooks "R-1953" (Abstract-Expressionism, Second Prize: $1,000)
Hedda Sterne "New York" (Abstract, Third Prize: $750)

Washington's 25th Biennial Exhibition Of Contemporary American Art At The Corcoran Gallery Of Art

Loren MacIver "The Street" (First Prize)
Fritz Glarner "Recreational Painting No. 79" (Second Prize)
Josef Albers "Homage To The Square" (Third Prize)

New York's Guggenheim Museum Has Exhibition By Marcel Duchamp, Raymond Duchamp-Villon And Jacques Villon, Three French Brothers Active In The Modern Movement.

PASSINGS

FRANTISEK KUPKA, Czech painter who created first totally abstract work.

DIEGO RIVERA, controversial Mexican mural painter, dies at 71.

Rumanian sculptor CONSTANTIN BRANCUSI, known for the beautiful simplicity of his work, is dead at 81.

French Artist **JEAN COCTEAU** Designs The Paintings, Altar And All Other Decorations For A 14th Century Chapel In Villefranche-sur-Mer, A French Fishing Village.

books

James Agee
   A DEATH IN THE FAMILY

Winston S. Churchill
   A HISTORY OF THE ENGLISH
   SPEAKING PEOPLES, VOL. III
   THE AGE OF REVOLUTION

Kathleen Winsor
   AMERICA, WITH LOVE

Bernard Malamud
   THE ASSISTANT

Ayn Rand
   ATLAS SHRUGGED

Edwin Way Teale
   AUTUMN ACROSS AMERICA

Theodor Plievier
   BERLIN

Henry Miller
   BIG SUR AND THE
   ORANGES OF HIERONYMUS
   BOSCH

James Gould Cozzens
   BY LOVE POSSESSED

Dr. Seuss
   THE CAT IN THE HAT

Erskine Caldwell
   CERTAIN WOMEN

Kathleen Kenyon
   DIGGING UP JERICHO

Boris Pasternak
   DR. ZHIVAGO

Leonard B. Meyer
   EMOTION AND MEANING
   IN MUSIC

Robert Bolt
   THE FLOWERING CHERRY

Ian Fleming
   FROM RUSSIA WITH LOVE

James Thurber
   FURTHER FABLES FOR
   OUR TIME

James Baldwin
   GIOVANNI'S ROOM

Jonathan Griffin
   THE HIDDEN KING

Vance Packard
   THE HIDDEN PERSUADERS

Lawrence Durrell
   JUSTINE

Art Linkletter
   KIDS SAY THE DARNDEST
   THINGS

Isak Dinesen
   LAST TALES

Gerald Green
   THE LAST ANGRY MAN

Roger Vailland
   THE LAW

Pearl S. Buck
   LETTER FROM PEKING

Stuart Gilbert, editor
   LETTERS OF JAMES JOYCE

Fred Hoyle
   MAN AND MATERIALISM

Simone de Beauvoir
   THE MANDARINS

Kyle Onstott
   MANDINGO

Mary McCarthy
   MEMORIES OF A
   CATHOLIC GIRLHOOD

Trevor Huddleston
   NAUGHT FOR YOUR
   COMFORT

T.S. Eliot
   ON POETRY AND POETS

PRIZES

NOBEL

Literature:

ALBERT CAMUS
(FRANCE)

PULITZER

Poetry:

RICHARD WILBUR
Things Of This World

History:

GEORGE F. KENNAN
Russia Leaves The War

Drama:

EUGENE O'NEILL
Long Day's Journey Into Night

Journalism:

CHICAGO DAILY NEWS

National Reporting:

JAMES RESTON
New York Times

International Reporting:

RUSSELL JONES
United Press

Biography or Autobiography:

JOHN F. KENNEDY
Profiles In Courage

WHAT A YEAR IT WAS!

Nevil Shute
ON THE BEACH

Jack Kerouac
ON THE ROAD

William Hollingsworth Whyte
THE ORGANIZATION MAN

Edgar Preston Richardson
PAINTING IN AMERICA

Cyril Northcote Parkinson
PARKINSON'S LAW AND
OTHER STUDIES IN
ADMINISTRATION

C. Day Lewis
PEGASUS

Jean Kerr
PLEASE DON'T EAT THE
DAISIES

A.J. Ayer
THE PROBLEM OF
KNOWLEDGE

Max Shulman
RALLY ROUND THE
FLAG, BOYS!

Theodore Draper
THE ROOTS OF
AMERICAN COMMUNISM

Iris Murdoch
THE SANDCASTLE

Saul Bellow
SEIZE THE DAY

John Steinbeck
THE SHORT REIGN OF
PIPPIN IV

Langston Hughes
SIMPLE STAKES A
CLAIM

Chaing Kai-Shek
SOVIET RUSSIA IN CHINA

Irving Wallace
THE SQUARE PEGS

Marshall W. Stearns
THE STORY OF JAZZ

Françoise Sagan
THOSE WITHOUT
SHADOWS

William Faulkner
THE TOWN

Arthur Bryant
THE TURN OF THE TIDE

Richard Hoggart
THE USES OF LITERACY

John Cheever
THE WAPSHOT
CHRONICLE

Robert Paul Smith
WHERE DID YOU GO?
OUT. WHAT DID YOU
DO? NOTHING.

William Saroyan
THE WHOLE VOYAGE
AND OTHER STORIES

James Thurber
THE WONDERFUL O

Richard Mason
THE WORLD OF SUSIE
WONG

Laura Ingalls Wilder, author of "Little House On The Prairie," dies at 90.

John Van Druten, author of "I Remember Mama" and "I Am A Camera," dies at 56.

Gabriela Mistral, Nobel Prize winning Chilean poet dies at 67.

Nikos Kazantzakis, Greek novelist who wrote "Zorba The Greek" and "The Last Temptation Of Christ," dies at 74.

CAT IN THE HAT??? WHAT A BUNCH OF RATTLETRAP

Despite receiving many rejections from publishers because of strange pictures and peculiar rhymes, Dr. Seuss persists and gets a publishing deal for "The Cat In The Hat" which appears to have as much interest from adults as from the wee folks. "How The Grinch Stole Christmas" is also published.

New Cambridge Modern History Begins Publication.

John Dos Passos Is Awarded The National Institute Of Arts And Letters Gold Medal For Fiction Awarded Once Every Ten Years.

Farleigh Dickinson University Begins Publishing "The Literary Review: An International Journal Of Contemporary Writing."

Françoise Sagan

200,000 Copies Of Françoise Sagan's Third Novel In Four Years, "In A Month, In A Year" Hits Paris Bookstores.

Jack Kerouac's "On The Road" Gives Rise To The Words "Beat" And "Beatnik" As Popular Phrases To Describe The Beat Generation.

Britain's Colin Wilson Describes Great Writing As "A Combination Of The Microscopic And The Telescopic."

1957 ADVERTISEMENT

Coca-Cola ... Favorite of the World. *A famous Canadian resort inspires another interpretation from the talented brush of Jack Potter.*

AT LAKE LOUISE, TOO..."SIGN OF GOOD TASTE"...The instinct for pleasant living goes wherever pleasant people go ... and takes the custom of enjoying Coca-Cola with it. So good in taste, in such good taste ... in more than 100 countries today, the invitation *Have a Coke* is the recognized signal for one of life's unique pleasures.

SIGN OF GOOD TASTE

ON BROADWAY

CHITA RIVERA & KEN LE ROY IN LEONARD BERNSTEIN & STEPHEN SONDHEIM'S **WEST SIDE STORY,** ALSO FEATURING CAROL LAWRENCE & LARRY KERT.

Another Opening, Another Night

Robert Preston and Barbara Cook

THE MUSIC MAN

LOOK HOMEWARD, ANGEL
Jo Van Fleet, Anthony Perkins, Arthur Hill

THE DARK AT THE TOP OF THE STAIRS
Pat Hingle, Teresa Wright,

Eileen Heckart

AND THEN SOME...

ROOM AT THE TOP
By John Braine

ENDGAME
By Samuel Beckett

THE ENTERTAINER
By John Osborne

THE CAVE DWELLERS
By William Saroyan

THE WORLD OF SUSIE WONG
By Richard Mason

JAMAICA
By Harold Arlen &
E.Y. Harburg (music & lyrics);
E.Y. Harburg & Fred Saidy
(book)

A VISIT TO A SMALL PLANET
By Gore Vidal

Eddie Mayehoff (*left*) and Cyril Ritchard

- **The Thrust Stage Is Introduced At The Stratford Festival Theatre**

- **Most Successful New Comedy: AUNTIE MAME With Rosalind Russell**

- **Most Successful New Musical: NEW GIRL IN TOWN Based On "Anna Christie"**

- **Cost Of A Theatre Ticket: $1.15-4.50**

will be seen for not more than ... eight weeks in the John Os- ... Alix Jeffry.

WILL BE GOING!

1957 TONY AWARDS

OUTSTANDING PLAY
"Long Day's Journey Into Night"
Eugene O'Neill

OUTSTANDING MUSICAL
"My Fair Lady"
Alan Jay Lerner & Frederick Loewe

OUTSTANDING DRAMATIC ACTOR
Fredric March
"Long Day's Journey Into Night"

OUTSTANDING DRAMATIC ACTRESS
Margaret Leighton
"Separate Tables"

OUTSTANDING MUSICAL ACTOR
Rex Harrison
"My Fair Lady"

OUTSTANDING MUSICAL ACTRESS
Judy Holliday
"Bells Are Ringing"

OUTSTANDING SUPPORTING OR
FEATURED DRAMATIC ACTOR
Frank Conroy
"The Potting Shed"

OUTSTANDING SUPPORTING OR
FEATURED DRAMATIC ACTRESS
Peggy Cass
"Auntie Mame"

OUTSTANDING SUPPORTING OR
FEATURED MUSICAL ACTOR
Sydney Chaplin
"Bells Are Ringing"

OUTSTANDING SUPPORTING OR
FEATURED MUSICAL ACTRESS
Edie Adams
"Li'l Abner"

OUTSTANDING DIRECTOR
Moss Hart
"My Fair Lady"

PASSINGS

MARIA PAVLOVNA CHEKHOVA, devoted sister of Russian Playwright Anton Chekhov, dies at 93.

Sir Laurence Olivier

Receives Honorary Doctor's Degree From Oxford University

Sir Laurence Olivier

And His Wife, Vivien Leigh, Lead Protest Against The Destruction Of London's Historic St. James Theatre.

EUGENE O'NEILL

Dominates The Theatrical Scene With Prizes And Plays Running On And Off-Broadway:

Pulitzer Prize
Long Day's Journey Into Night

Nobel Prize
Long Day's Journey Into Night
(Only American dramatist to have won this most coveted award)

Drama Critics' Circle Award
Long Day's Journey Into Night

On Broadway
A Moon For The Misbegotten

Off Broadway
The Iceman Cometh

O'Neill's Play **A TOUCH OF THE POET** Scheduled For New York Production Next Year.

DISASTERS

Hurricane Audrey Leaves Wake Of Destruction In Her Path

Hurricane Audrey roars down the Louisiana coast making a shambles of towns in her path.

Property damage is in the millions.

Hurricane Audrey

Audrey struck without warning leaving thousands homeless.

The 300 dead are scattered over a wide area and it's days until the final death count is known.

WHAT A YEAR IT WAS!

BLIZZARD HITS THE MIDWEST

Hundreds of cars are marooned as a snowstorm blankets the south and midwest with drifts of up to 30 feet in some places and a death toll of 38 persons.

Kansas is among the hardest hit of the five states.

This transcontinental train is completely buried with more than 200 passengers marooned for over 48 hours.

The last of the snow is removed from the train.

GENERAL MOTORS

The GM Golden Anniversary Chevrolet

The GM Golden Anniversary Pontiac

The GM Golden Anniversary Oldsmobile

GOLDEN FIVE for '58

Presented here are five typical offerings of 1958 automobiles from our five car Divisions in celebration of the fiftieth year of General Motors.

They are automobiles that—to be worthy of this event—were dedicated to surpass their own traditions.

And, while each maintains its own personality, all five cars benefit — as does the public — from the combined ingenuity of their own engineering staffs and the styling, research, development and testing resources of General Motors.

From the General Motors Technical Center comes a steady flow of advanced engineering and design developments—basic betterments in transmissions and engines—new ideas in comfort and safety features—new concepts in styling and appointments.

It is this General Motors leadership which has created such outstanding values in the cars now ready for your inspection in the showrooms of GM dealers.

They offer you, we believe, the widest selection and the most satisfying motoring to be found today.

The GM Golden Anniversary Buick

The GM Golden Anniversary Cadillac

FROM THE PROGRESS OF THE PAST . . . THE PROMISE OF THE FUTURE

1957

NUCLEAR FALL-OUT

Radioactive Material Spreads Throughout Countryside As Fire Breaks Out In The Windscale Pile Nuclear Reactor North Of Liverpool.

Kasli, USSR Is The Site Of A Chemical Explosion In Tanks Containing Nuclear Waste Spewing Radioactive Material And Forcing Evacuation Of The Area.

250 DIE IN RAIL DISASTER IN WEST PAKISTAN.

Fire Rages Through Home For The Aged In Warrenton, Missouri Killing 72 People.

Soviet Ship Eshghabad Runs Aground In Caspian Sea Killing 270.

Northeast Airline's Flight #823 Crashes Less Than One Minute After Take-Off From New York's La Guardia Field Killing 20 And Injuring 50.

Tornado Tears Through Kansas And Missouri Killing 48.

July: Earthquake Hits Northern Iran Killing 2,500.
December: Earthquake Hits Western Iran Killing 2,000.
San Francisco Hit By Worst Earthquake Since 1906.

FASHION

French Flair Combined With Exotic Fabrics Creates An Exciting Hello To Summer

Bermuda is the site for the introduction of French designer Givenchy's new line of swim wear.

WHAT A YEAR IT WAS!

This suit has separate pants underneath the tubular sheath, a distinctive feature of these new swim suits.

Two novelty suits, one reminiscent of the 20's with its long-legged look, have been made to look exciting with a vibrant mosaic print and pants that can be rolled up to the more traditional length.

1957 ADVERTISEMENT

American Modern...

revolutionary idea of freedom in fashion

your light and lovely underline...

Skippies
by
Formfit

This is the girdle
that states the case
for freedom in fashion
so beautifully, so very
eloquently, that American
women have voted it their
favorite. And small wonder,
because Skippies slim
and trim with the gentlest
touch . . . never a bit of
boning or heavy fabric to
hinder or hamper. See what
freedom and comfort
Skippies will give to you
. . . be fitted at your
favorite store.

Formfit

137

Balmain
Unveils
His New
Spring Line

According to French designer
Pierre Balmain, suppleness is the
word for Spring fashion using crepe, muslins and jerseys.

A light jersey dress falls into soft flounces.

A sumptuous evening gown of tulle over satin, set off with a stunning diamond necklace and earring set, makes this ensemble fit for a royal wedding.

A lovely silk chiffon strapless evening gown with a vibrant floral design.

1957 ADVERTISEMENT

in MIDNIGHT
fragrance

A. DeLuxe Set, 5 items, $7.

B. Cologne and Dusting Powder Set, $3.

C. Beauty Trio, $5.

D. Glamour Set, $1.

E. Permastick Lipstick, $1.10.

F. Foaming Bath Salts, $2.50.

G. Spray Mist—Cologne Concentrate, $2.

H. Perfume Vial, $1.50.

I. Bath Soap, $1.50.

J. Dusting Powder Mitt, $1.25.

K. Hand & Body Lotion, $2.

L. Perfume, 1 oz., $7.50.

All prices plus tax.

to tell her what she already knows...give her

CHRISTMAS GIFTS

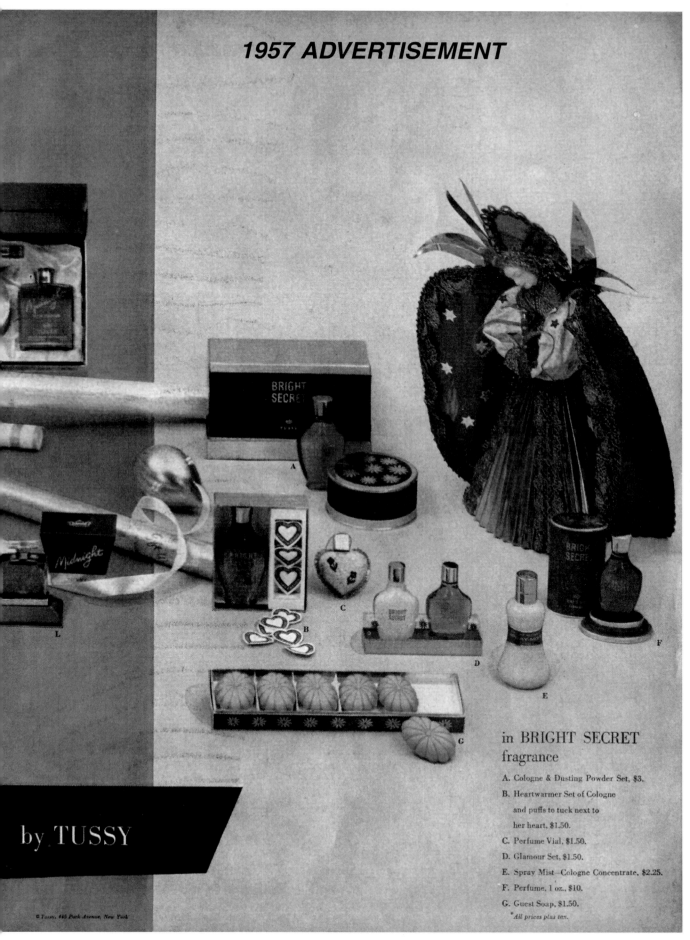

in BRIGHT SECRET
fragrance

A. Cologne & Dusting Powder Set, $3.

B. Heartwarmer Set of Cologne
   and puffs to tuck next to
   her heart, $1.50.

C. Perfume Vial, $1.50.

D. Glamour Set, $1.50.

E. Spray Mist—Cologne Concentrate, $2.25.

F. Perfume, 1 oz., $10.

G. Guest Soap, $1.50.

*All prices plus tax.

by TUSSY

© Tussy, 445 Park Avenue, New York

Stars And Socialites Model Fashions Unveiled At Recent Charity Ball At The Palm Beach Estate Of Mrs. Horace Dodge, II

A floppy hat to keep the sun off her oh so delicate face.

The hostess models this beautiful organza ball gown.

Lesley Cunningham wears a romantic bouffant dress of white organza.

A picture hat completes the ensemble.

Ann Miller looks smashing in her silk gown printed with huge blossoms, the back plunging to the waist.

Rita Moreno's strapless gown with a matching coat has a Grecian motif and is quite stunning.

1957

Exactly 10 Years After Dior's "New Look" Dominated The Fashion World, The Chemise Or "The Sack" Is Introduced By French Designers Givenchy And Balenciaga. Shaped Like A Giant Almond With Sleeves, And Obscuring The Silhouette, American Women Complain That The Sack Dress Is Hard To Iron While American Men Complain About The Lack Of Sensuousness.

The Styles Vary From The Scrubbed Pat Boone White Buck Look To The Beatnik Look Spawned By The Publication Of Ginsberg's Howl Consisting Of Khaki Pants, Sweater And Sandals While Jack Kerouac's On The Road Triggers Increased Sales Of Blue Jeans To Teenagers.

Pierre Cardin
Unveils His First Complete Collection.

Light Loosely-Woven Fabrics With Bold Patterns In Deep Red, Orange, Yellow, Blues (Sapphire And Cobalt) And Green Are The Most Popular Colors With Shades Of Brown Competing With Blacks For Evening Wear.

> *The Three-Piece Ensemble Is Quite Popular In All Price Ranges Consisting Of Dresses With Matching Jackets Or Cardigans.*

"COCO" CHANEL
RECEIVES THE NEIMAN-MARCUS GOLDEN ANNIVERSARY AWARD FOR HER GREAT INNOVATIONS THAT EMANCIPATED THE FEMININE SILHOUETTE AND FOR HER EXQUISITELY-SCENTED CHANEL NO. 5 PERFUME.

Brigitte Bardot, Clad In A Bikini, Stars In "And God Created Woman" Heating Up Demands For Swimsuits.

BRITISH COLUMBIA INTRODUCES COLLECTION OF CRAZY HATS FOR SPRING

This one is appropriately called a "Double Header."

One of the models from the Chinese YWCA in Vancouver wears "the biggest hat in the world."

Hey lady...is that a chicken on your head?

This one is called "Chicken With A Cigarette" and that's no clucking matter.

An oversized straw picture hat trimmed in giant flowers.

This one is made of stiff lace with black velvet ribbon running through it.

The Millinery Institute Of America Presents Its Spring Collection

A tall helmet of baby orchids trimmed with grapes and velvet leaves.

This large sailor is covered with silk roses and stems.

An off-the-face turban draped with a long chiffon scarf.

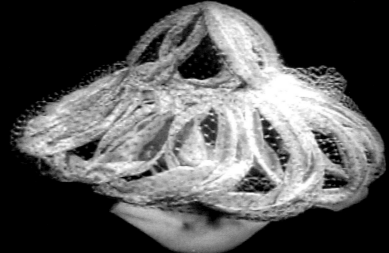

"Easter On Fifth Avenue" is the name of this casino circle of satin ribbon with straw braid.

Here's What The Experts Say About Wearing High Heels:

TWO HEELS UP

- Physically And Psychologically Beneficial;

- High Heels Throw The Weight Onto The Heel Instead Of The Toe;

- Eliminates Slouching;

- Produces More Healthy Breathing;

- Adds Inches To The Bust;

- Men Love Long Legs And Heels Give The Impression Of Greater Leg Length.

TWO HEELS DOWN

- Produces Bow Legs And Knock Knees And The Anti-Cruelty League Would Protest Loudly If Men Tried To Put Animals Into Such A Contraption.

The longer, more tapering line in a pinpoint-toe flat. The soft white kid is set off by a gold Puritan buckle. $12.95

Shoes

Shoes Are Fancy With Sharply Pointed Toes And Range In Fabrics From Striped Linen, Flowered Silk Crepe And Satin to Velvet And Lace.

Smooth-calf pump with new low back, white underlay, tiny buckle on vamp. Needle-point heel is unbreakable. $19.95

Rosebud-printed leather with linen sides, high-rising tongue and buckled vamp, curved Louis heel. $17.95

Mottled silk-print pump with slim teardrop toe, bright jewel at center vamp. Mid-heel and collar are of blue kid. $14.95.

Spectator calf teamed with gray kid, has high peaked throat-line and small tie at vamp. $12.95

Ascot-gray calf pump with high pointed vamp, defined by white striping, has a curved Louis heel. $18.95

Suede pump, with striped silk Edwardian tie, has the important needle toe, low back and Louis heel. $18.95

Deep red dress with matching jacket.

A bright red knitted wool suit with a printed silk blouse in shades of red and gold.

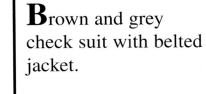

Brown and grey check suit with belted jacket.

Red tweed suit with matching handbag and beret.

Moss green jersey dress with matching cropped jacket. ($69.95)

Black tweed with sable collar, slim skirt and straight jacket.

Sapphire blue tweed suit with straight jacket ($47.00) shown with a matching blue silk blouse. ($10.00)

Light blue silk coat worn just above the knees sweeps backward into a light flair.

Basic black wool suit, slim skirt, lightly fitted jacket and off-the-neck collar.

Black silk polka-dot dress with bubble skirt and soft tie at the neck can be worn with a matching white wool cardigan (inset).

Black sheath with tunic length overskirt.

Basic sheath dress shown in black jersey (right) and red wool jersey (top).

Two-piece light pink wool crepe dress with pleated skirt and overblouse softly cinched at the waist.

PASSINGS

Christian Dior, Creator Of The Revolutionary "New Look," And Recipient Of France's Legion Of Honor Decoration For Breathing New Life Into France's Fashion Industry, Dies At 52.

SALE $1.57 EA.

STURDY TWEED RUGS

SAVE 41¢ Take 'em home for every room. You can't afford to miss this bargain. Cut pile tweed rugs of viscose and acetate. Latex back; fringed ends. 25" x 37". Gold, Aqua, Red, Green, Pink, Grey. Reg. $1.98 each.

SALE 2 FOR 97¢

LUXURIOUS CANNON BATH TOWELS

SAVE 41¢ Just try to match this terrific value anywhere. Fluffy, thick bath towels 22" x 44" in Cannon solid pastels or smart stripes. Regularly 69¢ ea.

SALE 97¢ COMPLETE

CAFE CURTAINS & VALANCE

SAVE 52¢ Brighten up the house with the newest curtain fashion at a great savings! Smooth cotton broadcloth. 50" over-all width x 36" length. Valance 70" x 8" included. Latest designs. Red, Pink, Gold. Regularly $1.49 pair.

Shoppers! Make **SMASHING** Savings

10 DAYS ONLY
Wednesday, January 9th, through Saturday, January 19th

on these eleven outstanding values

WOOLWORTH'S
January
$UPER-$ALE

Better hurry — they'll go like magic

...and all through January — storewide savings during Woolworth's month-long

97¢ SALE

Listen To The WOOLWORTH HOU

Every Sunday aftern Percy Faith, his Orch and Chorus, with outs ing guest stars, broadca "The Best in Music" full hour, *live* from York, over the CBS R network.

1957 ADVERTISEMENT

SALE $1.47 EA.
BEAUTIFUL 14" BOUDOIR LAMPS

SAVE 51¢ Amazing lamp value. Get them for every bedroom. Lamps with matching shades. White glass or gleaming brass color base. Regularly $1.98 each.

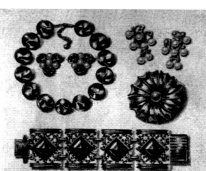

SALE 2 FOR 97¢ Plus tax
FABULOUS COSTUME JEWELRY

SAVE 21¢ Smashing value in jewelry for every occasion! Top-fashion necklaces, bracelets, earrings, brooches. Sparkling simulated jewels, rhinestones, gold color, silvery metals. These'll go fast, so don't wait! Reg. 59¢ ea.

SALE 97¢ PR.
DOUBLE RUFFLE DACRON CURTAINS

SAVE 52¢ Imagine Dacron at this low, low price! Dress up your windows with tier curtains. 60" over-all width x 36" length. Lovely fresh colors: White, Yellow, Pink or Green. Regularly $1.49 pair.

SALE 2 FOR 77¢
LARGE SILK AND RAYON SCARVES

SAVE 35% Get armfuls! It's your chance to own imported silk scarves without paying fabulous prices. Large 33" x 33" size in exciting colors. Gay prints. Regularly 59¢ each.

SALE 2 PR. FOR 87¢
FIRST QUALITY NYLONS

SAVE 31¢ Buy a supply! Exquisite full-fashioned nylons at a next-to-nothing price. Hurry in, they'll go fast! Newest fashion shades in 51 gauge, 15 denier. Sizes 9 to 10½. Reg. 59¢ pr.

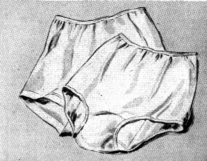

SALE 4 FOR 97¢
LADIES' FAVORITE BRIEFS

SAVE 38% Terrific reduction. Buy dozens! Full-cut acetate briefs; popular year round. With purchase of 4 save 59¢. White only. Sizes 5, 6, 7, 8. Regularly 39¢ pair.

Remember, there's also a storewide

97¢ SALE

going on for the whole month of January! Watch for 97¢ specials at Woolworth's all month long! (The 11 articles shown here are on sale only from Wednesday, Jan. 9th through Saturday, Jan. 19th.)

SALE 3 PR. FOR 87¢
MEN'S NYLON S-T-R-E-T-C-H SOCKS

SAVE 28¢ Buy 'em by the dozen for every man in the house! 100% nylon ribbed socks. One size fits sizes 10 to 13. Navy Blue, Brown, Charcoal, Black or Grey. Reg. 3 pr. for $1.15.

SALE 17¢ COMPLETE
IMPORTED CHINA CUP AND SAUCER

SAVE 37% At this low price you'll want a dozen of these beautifully delicate, expensive-looking china cups and saucers. Two shapes, three designs. Moss Rose, Violet or Columbia Rose. Reg. 27¢.

F. W. WOOLWORTH CO.

MEN "THE LOOK"

Suits: Small Glen Plaids

Sports Jackets: Huge Plaids (4 Buttons Not 6)

Hapi Coats Made From Oriental Silks

Handkerchiefs, Scarves, Ties And Ascots In Paisley Prints

Fake Furs

Cotton velvet Host Coat with rayon trim on shawl collar, cuffs and pocket available in dark wine, navy and black. $35.00

Dark grey shadow-striped wool gabardine Ivy League slacks with leather trim on pockets. $7.95

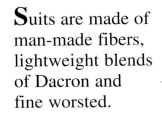

Suits are made of man-made fibers, lightweight blends of Dacron and fine worsted.

WHAT A YEAR IT WAS!

Buick SUPER 4-Door Riviera

When better automobiles are built Buick will build them

Roomiest hit in the Style Parade

(Step in and s-t-r-e-t-c-h
—it's the Buick SUPER—and what a dream car to drive!)

WE COULD give you facts and figures, chapter and verse, about the '57 Buick as the *roomiest* of America's best-selling cars.

And that's doubly true of the Buick SUPER pictured here.

Just step into a Buick SUPER—move your arms, relax your shoulders, cross your legs.

Then you'll know comfort that gets sweeter the longer you're there—and

styling that looks smarter the longer you stare.

But that's only the start of the thrills you'll find in this most completely changed Buick in history. The real excitement comes from performance that makes this the dream car *to drive*.

Power? You have it, in abundance—for you boss more might than ever gave vigor to a Buick before.

Response? Like nothing in an earth-

bound vehicle. For you have the instant action of today's new Dynaflow.*

Ride? Handling? Roadability? Braking? Try 'em and see!

Ask your Buick dealer for a demonstration—and for figures that make Buick your best buy today.

BUICK *Division of* GENERAL MOTORS

New Advanced Variable Pitch Dynaflow is the only Dynaflow Buick builds today. It is standard on Roadmaster, Super and Century—optional at modest extra cost on the Special.

Only Buick brings you this built-in "conscience"
SAFETY-BUZZER

—a simple device that's a great boon to your safety. You merely preset the miles-per-hour you want. When you reach that pace, a warning buzzer sounds. Drop below that pace and the buzzer stops. Standard on ROADMASTER, optional at extra cost on other Series.

Big Thrill's Buick

SPECIAL · CENTURY · SUPER · ROADMASTER · and ROADMASTER 75

SPORTS

Braves Edge The Yankees 4-3, Winning The World Series

Mickey Mantle ("The Switcher") in the dugout with Casey Stengel.

Pitcher Lou Burdette of the Braves pitches three victories making Milwaukee the new champions and is named the World Series' Most Valuable Player.

FOR YOUR DRYNESS,

YOUR HIGHNESS...

THIS FRESH, CLEAN TASTE!

● Whatever level you operate at—a dry throat is a dry throat. And a fresh, clean taste is what you need for it.

Not just "something cold", mind you . . . but 7-Up . . . the sparkling drink that not only tastes fresh and cool going down, but leaves your mouth and throat cool when you *finish* the bottle. Results? No stickiness . . . no come-back thirst . . . just a real *cool you.*

*You like it...
it likes you!*

Nothing does it like Seven-Up!

Baseball

SEASON HOME RUN KINGS

HANK AARON
(National League-Milwaukee)
44 Home Runs, 132 Runs Batted In
ROY SIEVERS
(American League-Washington)
42 Home Runs, 114 Runs Batted In

CY YOUNG AWARD

WARREN SPAHN
Milwaukee

MOST VALUABLE PLAYER

AMERICAN LEAGUE
Mickey Mantle
New York Yankees

NATIONAL LEAGUE
Hank Aaron
Milwaukee Braves

NATIONAL LEAGUE BATTING CHAMPION

STAN MUSIAL (St. Louis Cardinals)
.351 Average

AMERICAN LEAGUE BATTING CHAMPION

TED WILLIAMS (Boston Red Sox)
.388 Average

Highest Paid Ball Player TED WILLIAMS Signs $100,000 Contract With Boston Red Sox.

ROOKIE OF THE YEAR

AMERICAN LEAGUE
Tony Kubek
New York Yankees

NATIONAL LEAGUE
Jack Sanford
Philadelphia Phillies

GO WEST YOUNG MEN— AND THEY WILL!

New York Loses Two Of Its Major League Ball Clubs To The West Coast— The Giants To San Francisco And The Brooklyn Dodgers To Los Angeles.

JACKIE ROBINSON Announces He Will Retire From Baseball.

1957

18,000 Enthusiastic Fans Jam Madison Square Garden To Watch The Contest Between Home Team CCNY And Oregon State.

CCNY scores the first points.

The Northwest team scores again in this close game, much to the chagrin of this CCNY fan.

Some of the players take a spill after Oregon blocks a CCNY attempt at scoring.

The home team boys finally wrap it up, winning 58-51.

BASKETBALL

BOSTON CELTICS Beat ST. LOUIS HAWKS 4-3 For NBA Championship

•

MOST VALUABLE PLAYER OF THE YEAR
Bob Cousy (Boston Celtics)

ROOKIE OF THE YEAR
Tom Heinsohn (Boston Celtics)

NUMBER 1 SCORER
Paul Arizin 1,817 Points

•

NORTH CAROLINA Edges KANSAS 54-53 For The NCAA Championship

•

COLLEGE BOARDS

University Of Kansas' **Wilt ("The Stilt") Chamberlain** Is The Most Publicized College Basketball Player In A Generation.

With Several Years Of College Still Ahead Of Him, Seattle University's **Elgin Baylor** Is Deluged With Professional And Industrial-League Team Offers.

ICE HOCKEY

• **Montreal Canadiens** Beat **Boston Bruins** 4-1 For Stanley Cup Win.

• **S**weden Wins The World And European Championships In Moscow. Protesting Soviet Repression Of Hungary, The U.S. And Canada Among Some Of The Nations Boycotting The Tournament.

Question:

Why does Jack Kramer *crave* orange juice after a fast tennis match?

Answer:

His Body Wisdom tells him he needs extra Vitamin C and quick energy!

Jack Kramer, world-famed tennis star

Are you active, busy?
Then you need extra orange juice, too!

Stop and count—and you may find you cover as many miles per day as "Mr. Tennis" himself, and use up Vitamin C and energy just as fast. So when *you* have that same craving for a big, cool glass of orange juice, your Body Wisdom is telling you, too, to replenish Vitamin C and energy. You *need*

that extra juice, because—for busy, active people—having it with breakfast is just not enough.

Today, stock up on delicious Fresh-Frozen Orange Juice from Florida. It's rich in Vitamin C; it gives you quick energy. Make an *extra* pitcherful every morning!

This little can makes 4 big glasses!

Less than 5¢ a glass!

© Florida Citrus Commission, Lakeland, Florida, 1957

CHILDREN must have *extra* juice when they play hard to keep up energy and Vitamin C!

OUTDOOR WORKERS burn up Vitamin C and energy faster, must replace it often!

MOTHERS-TO-BE should double their intake of orange juice for extra Vitamin C!

FRESH-FROZEN ORANGE JUICE *Packed with Florida Sunshine!*

Althea Gibson First Negro* To Win Wimbledon & U.S. Nationals

Althea Gibson is congratulated by Darlene Hard after Althea wins the championship.

Queen Elizabeth herself presents the symbol of victory to this young woman from Harlem who is now the toast of the tennis world.

Sportsmen everywhere applaud her triumph and share in her moment of victory.

*Negro was the commonly used term in 1957.

TENNIS

Australia Beats U.S 3-2 To Win Davis Cup.

U.S. OPEN SINGLES CHAMPIONSHIP

Men: Malcolm Anderson (over Ashley Cooper)
Women: Althea Gibson (over Louise Brough)

WIMBLEDON

Men: Lew Hoad (over Ashley Cooper)
Women: Althea Gibson (over Darlene Hard)

LOS ANGELES WOMAN WINS AAU DIVING MEET IN HOUSTON

Paula Jean Myers of Los Angeles sweeps all five diving meets.

The beaming winner.

WHAT A YEAR IT WAS!

NEW RECORDS IN TRACK & FIELD SET AT THE NCAA MEETS IN AUSTIN, TEXAS

George Bell, Of Indiana, sets a new collegiate mark in the broad jump at 26′ 7″.

George changes shoes after his fantastic jump.

ICE SKATING

WORLD FIGURE SKATING CHAMPIONSHIP

Men: David Jenkins (U.S.)

Women: Carol Heiss (U.S.)

U.S. NATIONAL

Men: David Jenkins

Women: Carol Heiss

CANADIAN NATIONAL

Men: Charles Snelling

Women: Carole Jane Pachl

1957

FOOTBALL

DETROIT LIONS Beat CLEVELAND BROWNS 59-14 For The NFL Championship

IOWA Trounces OREGON STATE 35-19 Winning Rose Bowl Competition

NOTRE DAME Beats OKLAHOMA 7-0 Breaking Oklahoma's Four-Year Winning Streak

CANADIAN FOOTBALL LEAGUE CHAMPION (GREY CUP)

Hamilton Tiger-Cats Beat Winnipeg Blue Bombers 32-7

JIM THORPE TROPHY WINNER
Johnny Unitas, Baltimore Colts

John Crow, Texas A&M's All-American halfback is this year's winner of the Heisman Trophy.

WHAT A YEAR IT WAS!

"SUGAR" RAY ROBINSON Defeats GENE FULLMER, Regaining Middleweight Title For The Fourth Time.

•

CARMEN BASILIO Defeats "SUGAR" RAY ROBINSON, Winning The Middleweight Boxing Championship.

•

FLOYD PATTERSON Beats TOMMY JACKSON In New York Bout Retaining Heavyweight Title.

•

ARCHIE MOORE Retains His Light Heavyweight Title Knocking Out Tony Anthony In The Seventh Round.

•

Six New Members Are Elected Into The Boxing Hall Of Fame: CHARLEY MITCHELL, KID MCCOY, PACKY MCFARLAND, LES DARCY, BATTLING NELSON And JOHNNY DUNDEE.

BOXING

AUTO RACING

INDIANAPOLIS 500 WINNER
Sam Hanks (135.601 MPH)

•

WORLD PRIX GRAND CHAMPION
Juan Fangio, Argentina

RACING

CYCLING

TOUR DE FRANCE WINNER
Jacques Anquetil (France)

•

UNITED STATES CHAMPION
Jack Disney

•

WORLD CHAMPION
Rik van Steenbergen (Belgium)

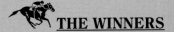 THE WINNERS

KENTUCKY DERBY
"Iron Liege"- Bill Hartack, Jockey
PREAKNESS
"Bold Ruler"- Eddie Arcaro, Jockey
BELMONT STAKES
"Gallant Man"- Willie Shoemaker, Jockey

Bill Munsey wins the Speedboat Gold Cup Race on Lake Washington in Seattle.

The First National Wheelchair Games Are Held At Adelphi College In Garden City, New York Including Table Tennis, Javelin And The 60-Yard Dash.

SWIMMING

Danish Olympic Swimming Champion **GRETA ANDERSON** Wins Coed Race Across The English Channel Covering The Distance In 13 Hours And 53 Minutes.

U.S. OLYMPIC WINNER BRINGS HOME A BRIDE

After weeks of pleading, American Olympic winner HAROLD CONNOLLY gets approval from the Czech government to allow him to bring his bride, Olympic winner OLGA FIKOTOVA, to the United States. They only have $.35 between them but look forward to a rosy future.

WHAT A YEAR IT WAS!

GOLF

U.S. OPEN
Dick Mayer (men)
Betsy Rawls (women)

MASTERS
Doug Ford

BRITISH OPEN
Bobby Locke

PROFESSIONAL GOLFER'S Lionel Herbert

Charles Sifford First Black Golfer To Win A PGA-Sponsored Event At The Long Beach Open.

CHESS

14-Year Old BOBBY FISCHER Becomes Open Champion Of U.S. Chess Federation.

VASSILY SMYSLOV Dethrones MIKHAIL BOTVINNIK'S 9-Year Reign As World Chess Champion.

BILLIARDS

World 3-Cushion Champion
Harold Worst, Chicago, Ill.

U.S. Open 3-Cushion Champion
Arthur Rubin, Brooklyn, NY

U.S. Pocket Billiards
Luther Lassiter, Elizabeth City, N.C.

World Pocket Crown
Willie Mosconi, Philadelphia, Pa.

BOWLING

54TH American Bowling Congress Champion
Jim Spalding, Louisville, KY.
Record Score: 2,088

FAMOUS BIRTH
Evelyn Ashford

TRACK & FIELD

London's White City Stadium Is The Site Of The Greatest Mile Race Of All Time When Four Runners In The Same Event Run The Distance In Less Than 4 Minutes.

University Of Pennsylvania Track Star Bruce Dern Resigns From Team Rather Than Shave His Sideburns.

The International Olympic Committee Votes To Add Volleyball And Archery To Its Sports Line-Up.

1957 WAS A GREAT YEAR, BUT...

THE BEST IS YET TO COME!